Sense &

Sustainability

Educating for a low carbon world

Ken Webster & Craig Johnson

ISBN 978-0-9559831-0-8
Typeset by i-site2020
Cover design and book layout by D Oakes
Front cover image One Day a Big Wind Will Blow by David Shrigley
Back cover image courtesy of Plenty Magazine
Book illustrations by Richard Crookes

Published by TerraPreta in association with Yorkshire Forward and InterfaceFLOR.
Contact publishing@terra-preta.co.uk

'TerraPreta' is the name for the rare black earths of the Amazonas region in Brasil. It is a soil enriched thousands of years ago by the then tribal peoples. It is fertile still. Scientists hope to recreate it for the modern world, remake tropical agriculture and sequester carbon at the same time. It represents a hopeful source of new relationships between humans and ecosystem. TerraPreta publishing hopes to use the analogy of a fertile source of great potential in its publishing activities directed towards systems thinking, education and sustainability.

TerraPreta Eco-policy
This book's footprint has been reduced by using print on demand and e-book formats, as well as diverting support materials to the website to reduce book length. Used books can be recirculated via Ebay or Amazon or via the publisher who will donate books to low income students and educators. Our emphasis is on shifting to digital formats (redesign) reduction (zero stock) and reuse. Using a major print on demand channel means that at present recycled paper stock cannot be specified.

To Peter Martin:
for his integrity, insight and a commitment to innovation
that enabled this book and much more besides

Contents

Why ESD/EfS programmes based on a 'do with less' approach are inadequate and often marginalised. Why we need something more satisfying and realistic. Changing perspectives described: from a 'cradle to grave' to a 'cradle to cradle' economy illustrated by *A Message from the Ants*, an extended storyboard for the accompanying powerpoint based on the work of William McDonough and Michael Braungart.
The role of frameworks for thinking discussed, why 'worldviews' matter and how they can help in EfS/ESD.

How did we get here? The strength of the mechanistic and linear 'take-make-dispose' worldview a legacy of industrialisation. The sustainability choices: matching economy with ecology. Five routes out but many are controversial. Consequences of existing ESD/EfS thinking and its limitations. Missing the big picture the Prisoners Dilemma, Jevons' Paradox, the Emptiness of Affluence and how more choice can turn out worse. Less bad is not good-more on the 'cradle to cradle' worldview, business and sustainability.

How the world is changing the end of the era of cheap energy and the impacts of climate change. How the linear worldview has influenced how we see change. Why we need to understand 'tipping points' and the role of feedback loops: change can be sudden. The story of the lily pond. The disconnected citizen, or the limits of just telling the facts. Sustainability in a 'what about me?' Society. How we can't shop our way to sustainability. The rebirth of community: transition towns

Why business is leading. Clean tech and the green collar economy on the move. A question of design. Examples of cities, products, processes: Dongtan, Masdar, InterfaceFLOR working with a closed loop, Nature inspired model. An aspiring low carbon region: Yorkshire&Humber, England. Principles of a sustainable economy explored. Service not goods, radical resource efficiency, biomimicry, restoring natural capital. Shouldn't education be a part of this? Exciting ideas and prospects from business but a 'greenwash' raincheck.

Pressure for change from grassroots and changing understanding of science, systems, teaching and learning added to innovative business. How a 'systems thinking' worldview is becoming 'resonant' and how it can promote the effective work of schools and colleges facing transition to a low carbon economy. Campus, curriculum and community prompts and discussion. Sustainable Schools. School gardens, living machines, green buildings to zero input farming and vertical farms examples. Why it's big picture not bolt-on.

A low carbon economy and a systems perspective will not leave schools and colleges unchanged as institutions. Stages towards a sustainable school. Individualised learning and community learning networks. 'Closing the loop' in nature, business and learning. An eco-restorative school? Discussion of the responsibilities of educators towards learners. Sustainable develoment is not a destination but a journey, and how frameworks for thinking help us on our way. Why we must be building cathedrals not just cutting stones.

An illustrated and concise summary of the main arguments. A low carbon economy based on the closed loop economy will draw its insights from Nature and systems thinking. Describes a coming together of several forces for change which will mean a change in perspective, or worldview, from which education for sustainability can draw a lot of strength and direction, as well as participate wholeheartedly. Six pointers to what to change in the here and now.

Foreword

by Jonathon Porritt

Jonathon Porritt is Founder Director of Forum for the Future www.forumforthefuture.org.uk, Chairman of the UK Sustainable Development Commission www.sd-commission.org.uk; and author of 'Capitalism as if the World Matters'; Revised Edition 2007, Earthscan – available through Forum for the Future website

I used to be a teacher. Ten years in a West London Comprehensive in the 1970s and 80s. There was not a lot of 'green thinking' around in those days, although my very supportive Head Teacher never objected to the odd outbreak of environmental activism! But she would be astonished at what's already beginning to happen within our schools, let alone at the 'bright green revolution' that is about to sweep over them.

And we really should be celebrating what's already happening. Over the last five years or so, the Department for Schools, Children and Families has set about re-thinking exactly what 'education for sustainable development' really means. The Sustainable Schools initiative, organised around the three C's of 'Curriculum, Campus, and Community', has been enthusiastically supported by countless schools and individual teachers, as has the Eco-Schools initiative. The National College for School Leadership has put sustainable development at the heart of its leadership mission, and the Qualifications and Curriculum Authority is constantly looking at ways of making the curriculum at every level more closely aligned with today's most pressing environmental and social challenges.

But that's just the starting point for Ken Webster and Craig Johnson. Their inspiration comes much more from a generation of thinkers and practitioners who have redefined the challenge in terms of *conflicting world views*. Unless we change some of the dominant assumptions (and dominant metaphors) that underpin our model of progress and economic development, the current 'reforms' we're introducing (invariably on a 'too little, too late' basis) will never do anything other than slow the pace of destruction.

And, well-worn cliché though it may be, we really are running out of time. The Intergovernmental Panel on Climate Change (the principal scientific advisors to world leaders in this area) tell us that we have no more than 15 years to build the foundations of the kind of very low-carbon economy we need if we are to avoid the worst impacts of accelerating climate change. The required shift, from grudging incrementalism to wholesale transformation, has massive implications for everyone involved in education today – and especially for the young people who will have to cope with such a different world. As David Orr puts it:

Foreword

"We need to equip our students with the practical skills, analytic abilities, philosophical depth and moral wherewithal to remake the human presence in the world. In short order, as history measures these things, they must replace the extractive economy with one that functions on current sunlight, eliminates the concept of waste, uses energy and materials with great efficiency, and distributes wealth fairly within and between generations."

David Orr is just one of the inspirational teachers whose insights have helped shape *Sense and Sustainability*. What they have in common is a passionate commitment to systems thinking, to re-interpreting our relationship with the natural world (seeing 'Nature as teacher' rather than as a bank of resources or a waste dump), and to schools as cross-disciplinary 'learning exploratories' rather than qualification-driven production lines.

As they set about persuading us of the need for such a radical re-orientation, the authors find themselves slaughtering all sorts of 'sacred cows' – including a lot of green sacred cows as well as the more conventional kind! Energy efficiency and recycling, for instance, may well be critical elements in the whole behaviour change agenda here in the UK, but it all depends on the overall context in which those policies are being implemented. If recycling is no more than 'a means of atonement', and reductions in energy consumption in the home are merely an excuse for taking ever more energy-intensive foreign holidays, then we are not really making much progress set against that bigger challenge!

By the same token, if some of our much-loved watchwords (such as 'Think Globally, Act Locally') are parroted with so limited an understanding of what personal responsibility in the global economy *really* means, then best not to utter them at all. There are so many seductive illusions around (particularly in the area of 'green consumerism') that a little bit of truth-telling with young people becomes all the more important – indeed, an ethical imperative. As the authors pointedly remind us, if its not possible to shop our way into happiness, we sure as hell won't be shopping our way into sustainability!

It's the speed of the required change that so many people find so daunting. Even the most progressive institutions engaged in negotiating the transition between today's suicidally destructive economy and tomorrow's more equitable and sustainable world (and it's great to see that Yorkshire Forward – the Regional Development Agency for Yorkshire and Humber – has been so supportive of the work done by Ken and Craig and of this publication in particular), have come to understand that we are only scratching the surface in terms of the scale of the behaviour change that is now needed. Though it is very dangerous to shove the whole burden of responsibility onto 'the next generation' (especially if we are doing that primarily to let us ourselves off the hook!), we have got no choice but to drive a far faster process of transformation across the entire educational world.

And that's the test. Ken Webster and Craig Johnson won't let anyone in education rest on their early laurels. Greener schools. Healthier schools. Extended schools. Connected Schools. Low-carbon schools. All good stuff – but if the end-game is 'the reinvention of modern society...by explicitly building a bridge from a sense of Nature into the late modern world', then we've all got a very long way to travel. Fortunately, for everyone involved in education *Sense and Sustainability* will make an excellent travelling companion.

Jonathon Porritt
July 2008

Introduction

Here's the essential break between lite green and bright green thinking: the reality is that the changes we must make are systemic changes.
Alex Steffen

Education for Sustainable Development(ESD)[1] is at its lite green stage. In practice, there is a lot of discussion about personal responsibility and commitment to reduce waste and consume wisely. Like Alex Steffen we accept that we need to evolve this into 'bright green thinking', a sense of remaking the world, of going beyond a some-times dispiriting 'less and less' prospect to something aspirational as well as sustainable. It also means refocussing on big picture, systemic, changes.

It is quite a task. For us to achieve it, there has to be a better framework for thinking. Luckily, there is. Innovative business practice, in fields as diverse as city planning, agriculture, construction and product design, is adopting a 'closed loop' (living systems) model. These firms and many community enterprises are illustrating a way of making sense of sustainability as part of a future which can be aspira-tional, coherent and comprehensible- and low carbon.

In Sense and Sustainability we hope to show how this 'closed loop' framework can help place ESD into the heart of a school's and college's ambitions for itself and its community. By explicitly mapping the core ideas of 'how Nature works' onto how education col-leagues and students see the modern world it can generate 'bright green thinking' – just as it has done for leading businesses like General Electric, Toyota and

Buckminster Fuller, the inventor of the geodesic dome, and author of the prescient Operating Manual for Spaceship Earth [way back in 1963] is something of a hero of ours. Anyone who has the nerve to announce himself by saying 'I always start with the universe,' gets my attention. He often asked, 'What is the most important thing we can think about at this extraordinary moment?' We can get onto the detail when we have the big picture sorted. We should also add that Number 9 in his ten leadership principles was 'Seek to Reform the Environment, Not Man'.

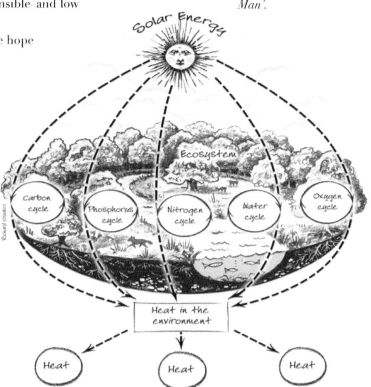

InterfaceFLOR. In this book we try to revitalise, bring together and extend work under an ESD heading while reinforcing the best of practice in participative teaching and learning–it shares a systems approach after all. For the first time, there is a coherent and increasingly well developed model which creatively engages with the challenge of a low carbon future and helps us to understand the unsustainable present. We hope the book will generate debate and test ideas around how we will live and work and provide for ourselves in an era of transition.

Sense and Sustainability uses exemplar businesses and innovations from around the world to reinforce its practical perspective, but its home base is the Yorkshire and Humber region in the UK.

An online supplement contains a strong selection of ESD activities for CPD work. A poster and a presentation in powerpoint format are available as a training and dissemination aid.

Most of the book's diagrams are available at the book's website to download and use within educational institutions. This book is available in print-on-demand and e-book formats via major online book suppliers and online at the *Sense and Sustainability* website as a series of downloadable chapters: http://www.senseandsustainability.com

David Orr[2] writes:

"The public, I believe, knows what we are against but not what we are for. And there are many things that should be stopped, but what should be started? The answer to that question lies in a more coherent agenda formed around what is being called ecological design as it applies to land use, buildings, energy systems, transportation, materials, water, agriculture, forestry, and urban planning. For three decades and longer we have been developing the ideas, science, and technological wherewithal to build a sustainable society. The public knows of these things only in fragments, but not as a coherent and practical agenda – indeed the only practical course available. That is the fault of those in the field of conservation, and we should start now to put a positive agenda before the public that includes the human and economic advantages of better technology, integrated planning, coherent purposes, and foresight."

This is where *Sense and Sustainability* comes in. It tries to bring into the ESD arena a simplified and coherent perspective, along the lines of Orr's 'ecological design' which stands a good chance of being intuitive to understand, and apply. The book provides focus for ESD

Seeing the bigger picture—the medieval adept glimpses the workings of the universe

practitioners with different approaches while being consistent with insights and activities emerging in the world of science, business and commerce–and in our understanding of how we think and learn.

The cognitive scientist George Lakoff[3] emphasises how new perspectives require different metaphors and 'frameworks'. Frameworks shape what we see as relevant and important.

Consider the dominant framework in the modern world: it sees 'Nature as Unlimited Resource (and Waste Bin)'. It is industrial development using 'take-make-dump' thinking. This is a linear, almost mechanical view of the world and in this perspective the thinking is about a 'cradle to grave' process with the industrial products and systems built on fossil fuels (buried sunshine!). People with the 'Nature as Unlimited Resource' framework of thinking understand sustainable development as meaning 'use less, waste less and recycle'. ESD is often seen as doing something to promote this end (with discussion focusing mainly on individual responsibilities and action).

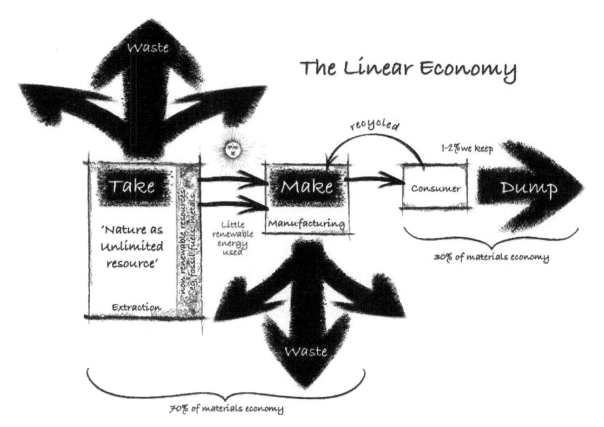

The Linear Economy

Waste

recycled

1-2% we keep

Take

'Nature as unlimited resource'

non renewable resources e.g. fossil fuels, metals

Extraction

Little renewable energy used

Make

Manufacturing

Consumer

Dump

30% of materials economy

Waste

70% of materials economy

But in this book we argue the case for another framework of thinking: 'Nature as teacher, Nature as capital'.

Most of the earth's natural ecosystems are driven by the Sun ('current sunshine'). In nature, 'waste=food'. Natural systems are self-sustaining and abundant. In healthy ecosystems competition and co-operation (participation) usually go together. Everything connects and closed loop, circular feedback mechanisms help to ensure a dynamic balance and continuity in the system.

Using the 'Nature as teacher' framework of thinking, industrial products and systems are designed and developed to *mimic* Nature – they are driven mainly by renewable energy sources and mimic the closed loops of natural ecosystems. Industrial products are designed in what is called a 'cradle to cradle' process. What end products cannot be composted (e.g. metals) go back to industry in a closed loop – as a valuable, easy to manage 'nutrient'. Waste is *designed out* using natural systems for inspiration. Education for sustainability becomes the

Introduction

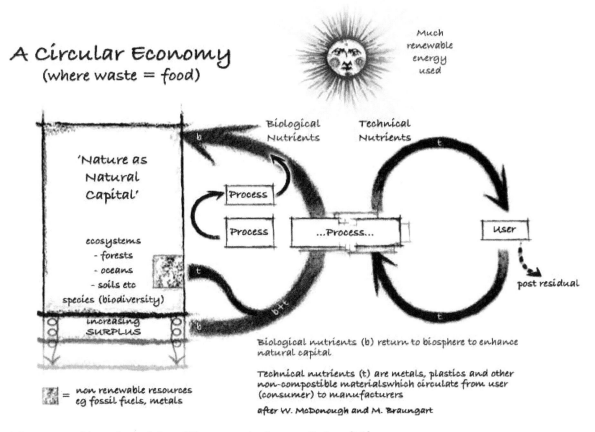

A Circular Economy
(where waste = food)

Much renewable energy used

'Nature as Natural Capital'

Biological Nutrients

Technical Nutrients

ecosystems
- forests
- oceans
- soils etc

species (biodiversity)

Process

Process

...Process...

User

post residual

increasing SURPLUS

= non renewable resources eg fossil fuels, metals

Biological nutrients (b) return to biosphere to enhance natural capital

Technical nutrients (t) are metals, plastics and other non-compostible materialswhich circulate from user (consumer) to manufacturers

after W. McDonough and M. Braungart

debate around how the insights of Nature can be best applied *explicitly* to a modern world in transition and to the processes of learning itself, which is also based on participation and feedback.

If this book was a check list – a sort of linear notion of course – it might come out like this

- See Nature and its processes afresh. Waste=food, diversity=strength etc
- Apply such ideas to the economy to make sense of sustainability (the Circular Economy – see above illustration)
- Give business and community examples
- Realise that living sustainably is something to contribute and aspire to: abundance by design
- Revisit traditional themes and issues in schools and colleges and design new enquiries

From this:

1. Develop learners insights on how Nature works

2. Develop learners insights on how innovative 'cradle to cradle' industry works

3. Develop learners insights about 1 and 2 using innovative participatory learning approaches

To this:

1, 2 and 3 share the same systems thinking - using 'closed loops' and 'feedback'

If it was one diagram it would look like this above

- Let go of the guilt
- Discover that the distance between humans and Nature has dissolved
- Engage continually

If it was a collection of references to various innovative writers and developers it would include William Stahel, William McDonough, Amory and Hunter Lovins, Mae-Wan Ho, Janine Benyus, Ray Anderson and Interface, Paul Hawken, Michael Braungart, Takio Kiuchi, and David Orr.

If it was a city it would be Dongtan in China, a floor covering called Entropy, and the phrases 'cradle to cradle' and 'the circular economy'.

The transition to a low carbon economy will be challenging but necessary. This book makes the case for a practical education for sustainability based on exploring and testing frameworks especially the ideas and innovations behind the leading edge of design, business and industry today. Inspired by understanding living systems, this new circular economy is transforming the sense of what a sustainable future might be. Education contributes most to the future of our young people when it opens up discussion on how sustainable can be aspirational: in our view, it needs to be about 'better and better' not 'less and less'.

We hope that *Sense and Sustainability* shows how the core ideas underlying participative learning, 'Nature as Teacher' and the 'closed loop' economy spring from the same sources, and transform, enrich and simplify how we approach our ESD work.

Ken Webster and Craig Johnson

Chapter 1

A Message from the Ants

*If you want to build a ship, don't herd people together to collect wood and
don't assign them tasks and work, but rather teach them to long
for the endless immensity of the sea.*
Antoine de Saint-Exupery

We need our utopias even if we can never quite get there. There is no sense in a sustainability which is framed around consumer guilt, and the atonement ritual of the recycling bin; a reality pictured as 'less and then much less' and as inevitable. A future where the wastfull world of the adults is meant to be resolved and cleaned up by their children, for the sake of the planet, will not be understood let alone embraced. It would be like asking them to show up at a party after midnight, offering them the few dried up snacks which are left along with a dustpan and brush to clean up all the mess. These responsibilities only make sense in transition to something far better. Education for sustainability must be a hopeful project, a series of questions about human intentions and actions, but framed by possibilities,

Figure 1.1: Below: termites and ants

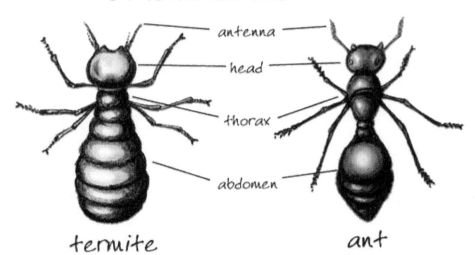

Differences and Similarities of Termites and Ants

antenna

head

thorax

abdomen

termite

ant

SAME
Both ants and termites are insects
Both have three body parts:
    head, thorax and abdomen
Both have six legs attached to their thorax
Both are about the same size.
Both are social insects and live in colonies

DIFFERENT
Ants have skinny 'waists' or thoraxes
Termites have straight antennae
Ants have bent antennae
Termite's antennae look like a string of tiny beads
Termite workers are blind

by the draw of imagining and creating an abundant, satisfying, more equitable future that nests within our supporting ecosystems. In short, like Saint Exupery's shipbuilding, educating for sustainability must be aspirational for it to succeed, just as it must be honest about the challenges of an imminent transition to a low carbon economy, for we have been partying long and hard.

What follows in the next section of this chapter is the outline of an illustrated story called 'A Message from the Ants', though it's a lot about termites. The fully illustrated and expanded A Message from the Ants, is available as a powerpoint presentation for use in continuing professional development (see www.senseandsustainability.com). The story describes how we got here and illustrates the sort of framework for thinking about the future which many leading innovators in business, product design, education and architecture are now using in their work. They are taking insights from living systems, from how Nature works, and applying them creatively in the modern world. In its unfolding, it offers an engaging perspective of our economy in transition. This framework is worth exploring as a way of bringing together the diverse elements of what is called education for sustainable development(ESD) and of shaping its future evolution. It's a good starting point for a *hopeful* education for sustainability.

Let's begin this story in the forest on the path to the lake. It's autumn and the leaves are thick on the ground, and still falling on this cold afternoon. For effect, and its not possible to resist, the banks of leaves on the edges of the path are the places to shuffle through, and listen, and look. Five months later in the same spot, on a warm spring day, the leaves have gone. The forest once inundated with leaves is clear, bar scraps here and there. Who cleared them all up? See figure 1.2.

Of course. The lake comes into view around a bend in the path, and a buzzing in the air reveals a recent death, a deer and a cloud of black flies.

Over time the deer releases its embodiment of energy – nothing is wasted as its body becomes food to over 130 different types of creatures from birds to beetles, maggots to bacteria. That's impressive. If the deer had been hunted and retrieved some of that embodiment would be called venison. Useful to us.

Or take the oak tree, a witness to the death of the deer and our observations. What is it useful for?

Ray Anderson, founder and chairman of Interface Flor the carpet tiling multinational said:

"As the forest's symbiotic relationships are understood, new organizing principles for industry will be revealed."

Figure 1.2: Leaf and lawn vacuum. Credit: DR Power Equipment

Figure 1.3: Dead deer. Credit: Luca Masters

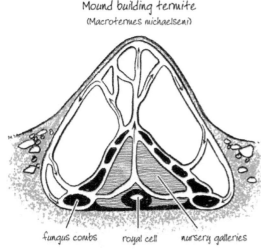

Mound building termite
(Macrotermes michaelseni)

fungus combs   royal cell   nursery galleries

↑ = direction of air movement

Furniture, fencing, roof timbers, decking, doors and windows... if we fell the tree and recover it. But there is another list: creating oxygen, holding the soil, helping to make soil, cleaning dust from the air, a home for birds which eat insects, a home for insects and worms which feed on dead and dying oak leaves, a shelter for other living creatures. A place for hundreds of acorns to grow... Correction: make that thousands upon thousands...

Surely it only takes one or two acorns to replace the old tree and perhaps add another (and oak trees can live for hundreds of years). How many acorns is that in a lifetime? Aren't so many acorns a waste? Of course not, the abundant acorn harvest is food for those other forest creatures. Nature is abundant, and often glorious. Have we forgotten or chosen to ignore that fundamental relationship, that in Nature, waste=food?

And Nature works, it survives, but is always changing – 3.9 billion years of experimentation. Creatures have come and gone but the whole thing has kept working. Perhaps it is the human, the ever so numerous and expanding human population which dislocates natural systems: a function of our numbers and consumption levels more than anything.

But for social organisation try termites and ants. These termites are not just good at turning cellulose into fuel (much to the envy of biofuel companies).

They are also cooperative – they have buildings, advanced fungus farming[1], air conditioning, nurseries for babies, cemeteries for the dead, soldiers, engineering workers, soil conditioning experts and lots of do nothing teenagers once in a while... and there really are lots of them in the world.

Figure 1.5 shows the estimated total weight of humans compared to the estimated total weight of ants and termites in the world.

And because they only live about a month imagine somewhat more than the current human population of the earth living and dying every month...

But the life and death of trillions of ants and termites isn't a problem to the working of the planet, its climate, its soils its oceans or forests. No one is saying there's an ant population crisis in the making (unless they happen to live in your house). They fit in fine, as do oak trees, cherry blossom and dead deer. They actually benefit the soils and the forest.

Ants work with the rules, if they didn't they'd be extinct. While waste=food, and so as long as the sun is in his empyreum[2] abundant life can go on forever–or as forever as humans can imagine.

Humans know this, indeed for much of our history we had to work with this wast=food rule, but even then it didn't always pan out. Sometimes humans took too much and didn't give back, so soil fertility was lost, or forests turned to deserts. Sometimes the climate changed too, disaster for the Tang dynasty in China and the Maya of South America[3].

But humans invented waste, stuff that

Figure 1.5: Humans and ants total biomass compared

wouldn't go away–metals, particularly–as in swords, ploughs, lead gutters and pipes. Actually much of this waste does disappear, it spreads slowly around in small particles so we don't notice. Heavy metals have spread throughout the oceans and end up in polar bears as they eat heavy metal-contaminated seals. Toxic industrial chemicals have also famously concentrated in human breast milk.

Humans really got into this waste-isn't-food-but-we-don't-mind-because-Nature-spreads-it-around-and-I-don't-live-where-it's-bad sort of habit when they found fossil fuels – buried sunshine. It was like finding a cupboard full of drinks, cakes and candies in the house. Here we go, party time.

Yes it fuelled progress with a capital P. The economy had become a catherine wheel spinning ever faster but leaving a swathe of smoke and sparks behind it, and not much else. This much stuff. But this much waste...

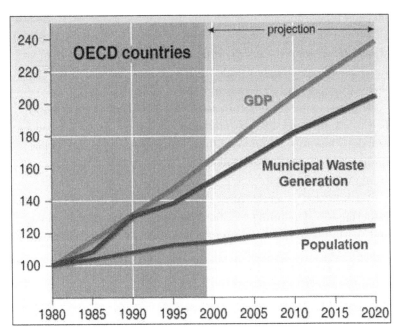

The economy became a waste producing system with some useful stuff thrown in. In short a bad design. Now the idea was that there should be no waste, after all the ants managed it and anyway the buried sunshine party was giving us headaches–enough waste to affect the climate – and the health of millions. This much we also know.

An obvious answer was to have less waste. Forget steam trains and big old cars, welcome light rail and compact dual-fuel wonders. Efficiency is a great idea if the energy saving isn't spent somewhere else, or by new consumers. Unhappily it has been. (see page 41).

Perhaps recycling materials is the key. But most recycling requires additional energy input and processing to remove contaminants. It

Figure 1.7: Relationship between growth and waste. Credit: Philippe Rekacewicz, UNEP/OECD/GRID Arendal graphics library (2004)

usually degrades the material in question so it becomes less valuable, meaning that the journey is still one way, albeit with detours. Much recycling is downcycling. And as people become richer they demand more products and recycling lags behind (see figure 1.7).

So the idea was to consume less, to make and choose products which are more durable, perhaps lead a simpler life all round... Sort of a lifestyle, moral choice.

Easier said if you are older, having burnt through youth and ambition; easier if you have had it all and wised up to appreciate the simple things, easier if you find using a ten year old computer on the internet a pleasant and diverting challenge... or own assets like a suburban house in a rich nation... or are not labouring in fields or factories for a pittance.

And anyway there are a lot of other people with money and degrees in psychology saying 'More is better', 'Buy stuff.', 'Stuff is happiness'. 'Stuff is freedom'. And the government says keep the economy growing, go on buying—we need the jobs, and taxes to pay for schools, hospitals, armies and so on.

There is a sense that none of these things can work, because they accept the idea of waste and so the economy remains a catherine wheel, a take-make and dump one way procession with some tidying up by the by.

Architects and designers like William Stahel, Michael Braungart and William McDonough have tried to restate the elegance and practical wisdom inherent in living systems to create a simple but profound sense of a new industrialism. Design as Nature does, remember the forest: Waste=food is a good start. The ants and termites are right.

Figure 1.8: Spiral of waste (after Mae-Wan Ho)

The dominant economic model of infinite unsustainable growth that swallows up the earth's resources and exports massive amounts of wastes and entropy

Everything which can be made to be non-toxic and composted should be. It's not waste then but food. For metals and other valuable non-compostable susbstances the loop needs to be closed by manufacturers reclaiming them in as clean and uncontaminated form as possible.

An example. Here's a new type of chair.

Figure 1.9: Think chair. Credit: Steelcase Solutions

It's designed in a new way. It's designed for use, yes, it's not toxic–it uses no toxic chemicals so it can sit in your room and not poison you bit by bit. It's also designed to be repaired easily, to be taken apart easily so the metals can be new chair pieces, or go back to be fixed up and part of a new chair straight away.

The fabric will compost, with no toxic chemicals left-over.... in experiments they've made the fabric edible (if you had to!). They will even take back the chair if you really think it's finished with.

Even better, why do you even want to *own* the chair, can't you just borrow it, rent or lease it, and then when it's time for a change the firm can take it back? After all people rent DVDs, cars and photocopiers. Why not chairs or carpets, or lightbulbs even? You don't have the problem of what to with it then and the firm gets all the lovely materials back again. Waste=food (but in a way ants don't quite understand). So in a 'circular economy' there are really two nutrient cycles, *biological* and *technical*. The illustration here is also a reminder of how we do things now.... Take-make-and-dump.

Most of the linear economy is waste as we know, and most of the traditional 'sustainability' discussion is actually not about

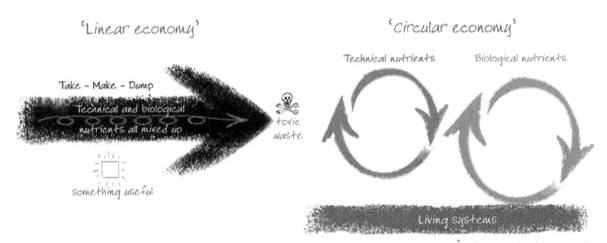

'Linear economy'

Take - Make - Dump
Technical and biological
nutrients all mixed up

toxic
waste

something useful

'Circular economy'

Technical nutrients   Biological nutrients

Living systems

sustainability at all it's about making the situation a bit less bad. It's a 'cradle to grave' assumption which dominates our thinking. It has a time dimension we ignore: it can't go on forever.

Here is how very badly designed the human made world currently is. This is a diagram of what happens when our food and water cycles get all mixed up. Note the linear flows.

Figure 1.10: The linear and circular economy compared

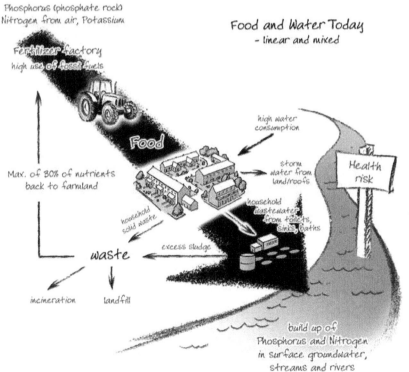

Phosphorus (phosphate rock)
Nitrogen from air, Potassium

Fertilizer factory
high use of fossil fuels

Food and Water Today
- linear and mixed

Food

high water
consumption

Max. of 30% of nutrients
back to farmland

storm
water from
land/roofs

Health
risk

household
solid waste

household
wastewater
from toilets,
sinks, baths

waste

excess sludge

incineration   landfill

build up of
Phosphorus and Nitrogen
in surface groundwater,
streams and rivers

Figure 1.11: Food and water today-linear and mixed

Figure 1.12: Food and water
tomorrow – closed loop and
separate?

But here in figure 1.12 is a diagram which shows how to eliminate most of these problems-by better design, based on keeping food and water separate and 'closing the loop' so that waste=food. No magic technologies are needed, no new sources of energy. Sustainability is always by design not by accident.

Instead of trying to make a bad system less bad why not try and create something positive? William McDonough suggests:

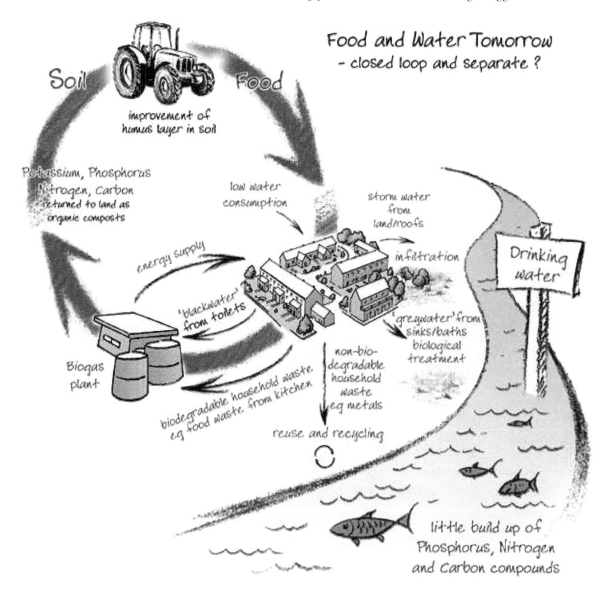

* Buildings that, like trees, produce more energy than they consume and purify their own waste water
* Factories that produce effluents that are drinking water
* Products that, when their useful life is over do not become useless waste but can be tossed on the ground to decompose and become food for plants and animals and nutrients for the soil; or alternatively, that can return to the industrial cycles as high quality raw material for new products
* billions of pounds (£) worth of extra materials for our use each year
* transportation which improves the quality of life while delivering goods and services
* a world of abundance, not one of limits, pollution and waste

Surely that's what we want? 'A world of abundance, not one of limits, pollution and waste'? Yet there is that question mark. Perhaps for some it isn't 'what we want.' This needs unravelling as so much ESD carries a moralising and unquestioned 'cradle to grave' perspective. This book makes the rather obvious statement that what makes sense, if we truly want 'a world of abundance', is moving towards a 'cradle to cradle' or circular economy perspective. It's not just the likes of William McDonough saying it. Here, for example, is the Chinese government...

"If we are to succeed...it is very important to develop a circular economy based on cradle-to-cradle design principles.[These principles represent] what China's central government wants to achieve."
Madame Deng Nan, China's Party Secretary for Science and Technology

"Visionary political leaders and responsible business leaders alike should work together . . . to pursue economic development on the basis of resource conservation and build a circular economy."
Hu Jintao, President, People's Republic of China

The main 'message from the ants': it can be done. Humans can be numerous, more numerous than now, living well, inspired by how Nature works in our economic activity, celebrating Nature, and maintaining its abundance and our human civilisation all at once.

Figure 1.13: RMI logo 'abundance by design' It's even trade marked!

We recognised that when we came to talk about closed loop models with educators it was the analogies and the stories which stuck in people's minds most readily. People seemed to find it fitted together or that they 'got it' this way. On top of the age old understanding that humans relate well to stories told at different levels, what we are 'getting' is the *framework*. So although *A Message from the Ants* sounds a too playful exercise at one level, a broad brush story telling or something a class of 13 year olds could understand, why not? This section of this chapter was based on the powerpoint version after all. It has been used that way. For an adult audience *A Message from the Ants* could easily have been condensed and its arguments more formally presented for the book. But that would miss other levels of the exercise. McDonough is not only the 'hero' of this narrative but some of the imagery is taken from his book with Michael Braungart *Cradle to Cradle Remaking the Way we Make Things* : the oak and the cherry tree, which we will meet again; the core ants story; the problems of recycling; design as human intention.

We can make sense of new frameworks and concepts by mapping the new onto other more familiar concepts: society as an ant colony; leaves and blossoms not as waste but as food; fossil fuels as buried sunshine; industrial products as nutrients; and the economy as a living system, not as a machine. It's a long way round to saying that the message from the ants illustrates another worldview, based on a number of key metaphors. Among them are *Nature as Teacher* and *Nature as Capital* (see chapter 4 for more on this).

George Lakoff and Mark Johnson, are cognitive scientists who claim that recent progress in their field has led to some world changing conclusions about how we think:

"The mind is inherently embodied. Thought is mostly unconscious. Abstract concepts are largely metaphorical. These are three major findings of cognitive science." [4]

Chapter 1

It takes a large book, *Philosophy in the Flesh*, to unpack what is within these few sentences but if Lakoff is right then we always approach the world through largely unconscious habits of thought. He argues that 'frames' are the mental structures that allow human beings to understand reality – and sometimes to create what we take to be reality. We can't learn anything very useful without acknowledging their pivotal role, without bringing frames, including these deep 'worldviews', into the open.

This may be quite a challenge as many of us have been brought up on the idea that the way to deal with uncertainty is to let the facts speak, to attempt to bring the universality of reason to bear and to work through to an objective position, however provisionally held. On the other side, there are those who see all attempts at objectivity fruitless and claim that people have quite different values and attitudes deriving from their cultures, histories and experiences. George Lakoff[5] concedes only a little to both parties – the analytical philosophers and the post-modernists (See reference for discussion.)

Just as there is no 'away' to throw waste, then if Lakoff and Johnson are right, there is no educating for sustainability outside of one or more frameworks for thinking. This means that education for sustainability based just on 'educational process', without a framework – like facts without context – makes no sense on its own. Or rather, the context will be there but because it remains unacknowledged and unchallenged it is therefore not subject to critical thinking.

Here then is the context setting for this book. Our intention is to contrast the mechanical industrial worldview with a living systems worldview. The former uses metaphors around machines and parts and proportionate linear relationships – where, for example, society is seen as just a collection of individuals and Nature is seen as an unlimited Resource and waste depository.

By contrast, people with a living systems world view see the whole as greater than the sum of the parts and where connections and relationships matter more than parts – they recognise that these relationships are based on loops and feedback. Here Nature is Teacher and Capital. Both the above worldviews are deep frames but not mutually exclusive in most people's minds. Lakoff suggests that few people are consistent in their use of frameworks – he also argues that consciously holding a particular framework does not make you right, it just makes it easier to argue your case.

"If one cannot think without mental patterns–and, in my belief, one cannot–it is better to know what they are; for a pattern of which one is unconscious is a pattern that holds one at its mercy."
Arnold Toynbee

What can't last won't last.
Beyond all political innuendo, the word 'sustainable' means simply that this or that way of doing things has staying power. We are now one hundred thousand years old. There remains a vast way to go, and it's clear the machine metaphor can't take us there. By depleting resources too quickly and piling up too much waste, we have already begun to hit the wall of ecological limits. That we are smarter than algae is a given. Whether we are wiser remains an open question.

Source: Robert Frenay Pulse: The Coming Age of Systems and Machines Inspired by Living Things

We adopt the living systems inspired, cradle to cradle metaphors as progressive and helpful (read more about them in Chapter 2). 'Systems thinking' can help clarify more than just sustainability issues for example, it has a lot to say about how change happens, the role of the individual in society, and how aspects of science operate (see Chapter 3). It also helps make the simple case that effective education is based on thinking coherently and critically – making better sense – as well as acting.

Walter Stahel, the father of modern closed loop thinking, was keen on the following story. In it, three stone masons were observed hard at work. Asked what they were doing, the first one replied that he was working his eight hour shift. The second said he was cutting limestone blocks. The third offered that he was building a cathedral.

It is the sometimes derided 'vision' thing once more. Meaning derives from context and the more it represents something aspirational the more likely it is to be done, and done well. Sustainability must be much more than saving on the school or college energy and photocopying bills, as it were.

The next chapters look in more detail at the journey to the present day and the challenges societies are facing. Divert to Chapters 5, 6 and 7 if you are happy with the basic argument and want to explore and share the fine art of cathedral building.

Chapter 2

Moving on – Recycling AND...

*Cradle to cradle design means that we can eliminate the concept of waste.
It doesn't support guilt language. It's not about reduction, avoidance
or minimisation. It's about abundance.*

Michael Braungart

That's a relief. Pass another iced bun. If Michael Braungart is right then a major focus of education for sustainability shifts. Imagine a thought experiment where all existing ESD programmes and environmental education were shorn of the 'guilt language...reduction, avoidance, minimisation.' How much would remain? Scary, or perhaps a reason to be cheerful, as guilt is such a demotivating force in human affairs. This, however playful, is an example of the power of changed perspectives, and the opportunity which follows is to investigate, and with increasing confidence, discuss what 'abundance' in a low carbon world might mean. The 'cradle to cradle' framework helps do this.

However, for all that Chapter 1 promises, we are not about to be landed gently onto this pleasant and bountiful shore by the riffling trade winds. Rather, the aftermath of the storm is running aground the vessel upon which we have built so much over the last couple of hundred years. In short, how did we find ourselves among such rocky shoals?

On machines powered by 'buried sunshine'(fossil fuels) is the equally short answer. Once freed from the limits of the cycles of the seasons, from the limited productivity of hand and horse, from the winds, the tides and flowing water, and the limits of the merely local by steam power, coal and later petroleum, we began to be comfortable that the energy slaves unfettered in burning fossil fuels offered more

Figure 2.1: 'Hold it from now on, only half a cup each!'
Credit: High Moon

Note: "Advanced" countries must first reconsider the size of their own share.

Chapter 2

advantages than less. The price of Progress was affordable. More input equals more output – hooray. Faster is better than slower at creating wealth – hooray.

This is a familiar linear, almost mechanical view of the world, drawing down a stock of resources, as this cartoon in 2.1 illustrates. People with this framework of thinking understand sustainable development as meaning 'keep going' but 'use less, waste less, recycle and share'. ESD is then primarily seen as being instrumental, doing something to promote and extend the life of this industrial model and extend its benefits (with discussion often concentrating on individual responsibilities and choices). Hence the chances that guilt and obligation are on the agenda too. It's characterised in mature economies as 'business as usual but greener and fairer.'

Sometimes this approach is also called 'green after gold'. The idea being that after a dirty period, growing economies can move onto cleaning up their act. Just like Britain or Germany in a previous century, China and India will have to pass through a dirty industrial phase before being economically rich enough to afford the costs of a cleaner economy. After all, so the argument goes, it seems to have worked well in the West.

So what is called sustainability follows by and by. Except that it isn't sustainability of course – cleaner doesn't mean green – if it's still based on more and more materials and energy being used overall and a shift of dirty industries 'offshore'. More than that, the existing capitalist system works – absolutely depends upon – endless growth in consumption and demand, and is thus inherently unsustainable. There are no limits in effect. It is as though there is no time dimension either. A microwave culture: I want it hot and I want it now!

Worse still: it isn't even an option fully available to the whole world. As the 2002 Earth Summit Jo'burg Memo puts it,

"[T]here is no escape from the conclusion that the world's growing population cannot attain a Western standard of living by following conventional paths to development. The resources required are too vast, too expensive, and too damaging to local and global ecosystems."

Three strikes and you're out? Won't work, can't work, yet it's still the default response to ecological problems among most of the world's bankers, politicians and journalists. Denial is obviously not just a river in Egypt.

From an educational perspective the more interesting question is why this Green after Gold mythology is not challenged more often. Perhaps because it is a convenient and encompassing mythology, concentrating on today's benefits, vaguely offering a better future, with a few silver bullet technological fixes thrown in: GM food, nanotechnology, nuclear fusion, the hydrogen economy. Perhaps it's because of an impression that there isn't much else around which is either a compelling or believable counterpoint. Perhaps because it is simply familiar, at least to the comfortable 20%, the golden billion of the world's population. Perhaps because it suits the folks in charge. As with all things, even ideas, power is a great aphrodisiac.

Five Ways to Fit – or how to match economy with ecology[1]

Nature as Teacher and the Circular Economy

Chapter 1's 'closed loop', nature inspired circular economy is one way of producing a fit between economy and ecology. If it's uncomfortable or seems idealistic then there are other possibilities. The first of them is so unsavoury it is rarely discussed.

'Drop off and die' – the Titanic lifeboats theory

In the face of far too many people, and too few resources, so the argument goes, the rich will pull up their ladder, turn surplus food into fuel-oil and wait, just as the people who had been able to secure a place on the life sustaining lifeboats of the Titanic waited, until the cold waters of the Atlantic winnowed the thousands struggling in the sea. It is doubly ironic that the rich were heavily over represented in the Titanic's lifeboats too.

The world is brought back into a balance by a reduction of people, though at a terrible cost. Apart from the immorality of it, it's idiotic as an idea if only for the fact that the global economy and environment, from which the rich cannot disentangle ourselves, will not outlast the most of us using every last lump of coal, spider crab or rainforest log. The rich will just starve and freeze in their lifeboats, to continue the analogy. There is no SS Carpathia about to show up with tea and blankets. Unless, of course, you believe in the Rapture or space aliens as rescuers.

The Great Change of Heart

In short, it's down to the individual conscience. The term 'lifestyle choices' soon comes to mind. Alex Steffen puts it this way:

"Why do good people keep advocating lifestyle change? Well, the hope is that small steps will lead to a big change of heart: that a tipping point will occur when the crucial can falls into the critical recycling bin, and people all around the world will awaken to the sustainability imperative, and then that, in some vague-but-direly-hoped-for way, this awakening will change everything and all will be well (and everyone gets a pony!)."

It rather depends on nearly the entire planet, as Alex Steffen also notes:

"agreeing spontaneously to all forgo the myriad pleasures and enticements of modern wealth and live in a simpler, perhaps truer way. This is what I think of as the Mythological Universal Conversion Event. Needless to say it hasn't yet arrived. If you still believe it's coming, that's fine: I don't."

And sadly, neither do we, based on the evidence that aspirations are almost entirely in the opposite direction – young people especially, from Siberia to Rwanda, all share the desire for a better life. Most won't listen to entreaties to live simply, nor should they, necessarily. Sustainability involves improving social capital and attending to social equity. Thus poor people by the billion would have the opportunity of a significantly higher consumption in order to maintain themselves and improve their communities. Change of heart or not, voluntary simplicity does not automatically address how energy or products are made, used, or disposed of in both developed nations and by the newly consuming classes in countries such as India and China. It is possible to live simply but still unsustainably. There is a groundswell of sympathy for a more authentic, meaningful and less damaging pattern of consumption in the West (see the New Realists p46). But it does not add up to sustainability while behind it is the massive impact and profitability of the unsustainable production, transportation, energy, food and construction systems upon which we depend and over which we currently have essentially no direct control.

A Return to Traditional Ways of Life.

Since modern, industrialized society is clearly unsustainable, there are those for whom the obvious answer is to go back even further to the way we lived before the industrial revolution, taking more than the wisdom and lifestyle cues of the small pockets of indigeneous peoples still relatively isolated from industrialism, but their methods too. While it might seem to work on a small scale it doesn't work for a planet full of people–there is simply no way it is productive enough to feed over six billion people. Already half the world is urban. And those with a vote won't back it this side of total collapse. While there are important lessons to be learned from the diversity of cultures and, say, land management techniques, husbandry and the sophisticated knowledge of plants and animals available in such societies, it won't add up to be globally sustainable. Nor did it do so in some romantic past, as Jared Diamond has eloquently argued in *Collapse* – human society seems very bad at living within eco-limits in any epoch of our history. The past is no haven for humanity.

Green after Gold

Already outlined in this chapter as the big player, its message is grow economically first and then tidy up the environment and improve welfare later–but its prospects are poor when it comes to fitting economy to ecology.

Assume for now that Green after Gold, 'business as usual but greener and fairer' is the dominant framework. It is built around a way of seeing the world with strong roots in the science of the Enlightenment and its linear and reductionist approaches. Let's see what emerges in ESD as a consequence of this mindset. Ahhh recycling!

Recycling for every occasion. It's often a major focus of ESD work in schools and colleges. Essentially, recycling looks to have a lovely closed loop identity, defying the linear assumption from the off, but most recycling is downcycling and narrowly conceived: far from 'cycling' materials at a high quality and with minimum additional energy or treatment the opposite effect is most often observed.

Material is degraded in quality and additional energy and refining are often needed, and the end result is unchanged – it is soon in landfill or the incinerator, 'recycling' having been a mere detour in its earthly and often toxic procession. End-consumer recycling misses 70% of the waste in the materials economy in any case[2]. A sobering thought. Although the UK's Waste & Resources Action Programme (WRAP) concludes recycling worldwide has a net environmental benefit this is not the same as saying it is part of an ecologically sustainable future. Less bad does not equal good. The underlying assumption is still linear. Take, make and dump (and err... tidy up some). At least it's a start, we all accept that.

Recycling is also a highly symbolic term and image. The word 'recycling' comes to mind very easily to young people and adults, let alone governments and is seen favourably. Much more so than the Rs of 'rethink and redesign', 'reduce', 'repair' or 'reuse' and this, despite the well known waste hierarchy which puts recycling pretty low down as an effective strategy.

This is a puzzle until, as Clive Hamilton and Richard Denniss point out, recycling from an end consumer standpoint is recognised as the only one of the Rs which legitimises further consumption[3]. The others clearly interrupt that intention. Recycling as we see it today can arguably be seen as a means of atonement for excess consumption, and is not perhaps intended to resolve the paradox of increasing production, consumption and waste on a finite planet but just to make it all feel less uncomfortable. Put it another way, why so much noise about the fourth down and so little about the first on this waste hierarchy diagram?

To which there are always loud choruses of 'but recycling, it's better than doing nothing...' Yes it buys some time. Figure 2.4 shows the progression of PET bottle recycling in the USA. Not much time... and even then the PET does not often go back into bottles as the quality is degraded[4].

Figure 2.2: Recycling loops

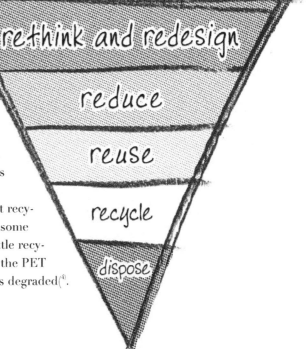

Figure 2.3: The waste hierarchy

rethink and redesign

reduce

reuse

recycle

dispose

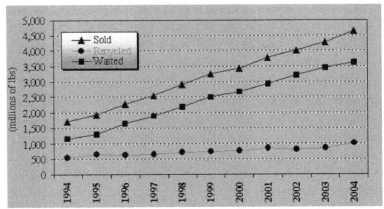

Figure 2.4: USA recycling not keeping pace with sales. Credit: American Plastics Council/Container Recycling Institute

It also seems strange that these choruses so often miss the obvious: it is not one choice or the other, it's recycling AND... It might even be appropriate to describe the first stages of a progressive ESD as 'recycling AND...' The answer to the question begged 'and what?' seems clear, and was laid out in Chapter 1. It's 'Rethinking' and 'Redesigning'. Waste=Food is waste hierarchy's 'Avoidance' in a circular economy. Top choice.

We need to reclaim the moment and spend less time in education assuming certain options are good or bad (then doing more of the 'good' ones). Instead, we need to shift to testing ideas within different frameworks and against the evidence. 'Recycling is a good idea' becomes 'Is recycling a good idea?' Context again. Education only exists inside the second formula, in the first it is mere Training. We are not supposed to be doing 'T'SD. Or are we? In our view, ESD is a context thing first and foremost, as these examples will confirm. It is back to the notion that moving on from 'lite green' requires systemic change and an understanding of it.

Eco efficiency and Jevons' Paradox

Eco efficiency or 'doing more with less.' This is usually seen to be the epitome of a more sustainable approach and it is one for which schools and colleges are often praised. It is rarely criticised, but consider something called the Jevons' Paradox, which could be described as an example of putting eco-efficiency in context. Jevons' Paradox is, technically, the rebound effect in consumption when technology improves efficiency. It's best told through example.

Figure 2.5: W.S. Jevons

"Let's magically double the average fuel economy of America's cars and trucks. Gasoline demand would drop immediately by 50%. This would affect the supply-demand equilibrium of gasoline, reducing its price significantly. However, with dramatically lower gas prices, many people would choose to drive more than they had in the past – this is the 'rebound', where some of the energy savings provided by gains in efficiency are negated by the corresponding effect on energy prices. Clearly, a 50% drop in gas prices won't result in the average American doubling their driving, as would be required to completely remove the efficiency gains in this scenario. People only want to drive so much. Studies suggest that it erases perhaps 10%-30% of the gains. If Jevons' Paradox, via the rebound effect, only negates 10%-30% of gains from improved efficiency, then efficiency appears to be a very viable policy option to reduce energy consumption? Not so fast... Consider the cascading effects in the energy-consumer system: when we save energy because of improved efficiency, we also save money. What do we do with that money? Chances are that most or all of it is spent on goods and services, and that these reflect energy consumption in some form. Whether we spend our savings on a trip to Hawaii, a new coffee table, or merely a plastic bauble, that expenditure reflects energy consumption. The exact form of energy consumed, as well as the relative quantity of energy consumed compared to energy initially saved via an improvement in efficiency is difficult to quantify, but in aggregate these two may be roughly equal. This is the 'shadow' rebound effect. The 'direct' rebound effect may be only 10%-30%... but it is possible that the true rebound effect approaches 100% when this 'shadow' is accounted for."[5]

This is a perfect example of the limits to many current ESD programmes, in which it is assumed energy or materials efficiency is a good option, because these ESD programmes isolate the thinking behind the assumption. But in reality, to quote Jeff Vail, an energy intelligence analyst for the US government, 'we must be careful not to present efficiency as a standalone panacea, but rather to spur debate of systemic solutions of which efficiency is a key part'.

Here is a more extended way of putting this crucial argument, from Amory and Hunter Lovins and Paul Hawken:

"Without a fundamental rethinking of the structure and the reward system of commerce, narrowly focused eco-efficiency could be a disaster for the environment by overwhelming resource savings with even larger growth in the production of the wrong products, produced by the wrong processes, from the wrong materials, in the wrong place, at the wrong scale and delivered using the wrong business models. With so many wrongs outweighing one right, more efficient production by itself could become not the servant but the enemy of a durable economy."[6]

Oops! The Take-Make-Dump 'worldview' likes to see problems and solutions in isolation – like efficiency or recycling – and in failing to make sense of it *fails to discuss sustainability at all.* Context matters – and none more so than with the assumption that individual actions can add up to significant change, whatever the context. It is the same sort of confusion which emerged with efficiency: adding up the particular – the individual, the school or college – does not create the general case. Different rules apply. This blindness has afflicted so much ESD to the current time. Here is a core example.

'Think Globally-Act Locally' – the Prisoners' Dilemma

'Think Globally-Act Locally' is one of those easy to digest, easy to repeat phrases we have been hearing for decades. But many of the assumptions about human behaviour when 'acting locally' have a deep flaw to them. It is called the 'collective action problem' or the Prisoners' Dilemma.

The 'think global, act local' slogan is often followed by assertions to the effect that 'if we all …. saved paper/turned the tap off/ walked to school' it would make an overall difference. The challenge, given that we agree on the aim of avoiding ecosystem and biodiversity collapse, is why we don't then act in our own interests. Surely this is irrational behaviour, goes the argument, so let's all be sensible. However, Joseph Heath and Andrew Potter in their book *The Rebel Self*[7] explain:

"In our view, almost all environmental problems, most of the pathologies of globalization, and the most unattractive features of the market economy are all forms of the prisoner's dilemma. Essentially, the prisoner's dilemma shows how two individuals, acting in their own self-interest but bearing no malice toward one another, can wind up producing an outcome that is collectively disastrous. Yet even when they recognize that their actions are self-defeating, they have no incentive to stop.

The cause of the prisoners' dilemma, however, is not individual greed or avarice. Often it is merely the decentralization of decision-making that can lead individuals into these sorts of collective action problems. Local governments, for instance, often get locked into these sorts of dysfunctional behavior patterns, when they compete with one another by offering tax breaks to businesses, or by offering cheap land to developers. The mere fact that we all share the same 'global' evaluation of how we would like things to be does not mean that any of us are willing to take the steps necessary to get things that way. Thinking globally is therefore not much of a solution to anything, because people still respond to incentives, and as long as the incentives remain local, the chances of a collective action problem blocking any progressive efforts are very high."[7] See The Prisoners' Dilemma box.

It seems disconcerting that many educators fail to deploy this argument – until the influence of a reductionist 'frame of mind' is factored in to the equation. This framework implies that adding up individual choices is a simple matter, that these choices are not contingent but are taken by free, rational actors; that these are the key choices.

The problem, like many others, is then devolved and projected as a moral one for individuals not necessarily a systemic one for those who set the 'rules of the game.' The enabling role of systemic incentives is largely missed as is the disabling role of local ones. We are back to guilt once more.

What about local community and individual action?

Local action matters very much, as does individual action. Its importance is not so much the action itself, it's more that it brings the possibility of a sustainable world through its impact on changing *thinking*, by illustrating the possibilities, the benefits and strengths of different models, not to mention the strength of feeling about change on the body politic. Systemic problems require systemic solutions.

The Prisoners' Dilemma

Conventionally illustrated by means of an example involving two prisoners trying to decide whether or not they should inform on one another. These two prisoners find themselves in jail in separate cells awaiting trial, having been caught and charged for their participation in the same crime. The police go to each of the prisoners in turn and offer them the same deal – if you inform on your friend, we will see to it that you get a shorter sentence. Both men know that precisely the same deal will have been offered to their partner-in-crime; however, neither man knows for certain, or has any way of finding out, which decision the other will make. This is the crux of the problem – the outcome of either prisoner's decision depends in part on the decision made by the other prisoner, which decision the other has no way of knowing for certain in advance.

There are four possible outcomes. If they both stick to their story and refuse to talk (ie they 'co-operate' with one another), the law will have a hard time pinning anything on either of them and therefore they will both benefit. They will both end up with, at worst, a minimal sentence. However, each prisoner knows that if he 'co-operates' while the other 'defects' (ie, turns informer), he will end up losing heavily, because he will be doing the sentence for both of them – this outcome is known as the 'sucker's pay-off'. Likewise, the other prisoner is aware that the same thing could happen to his disadvantage, if he keeps quiet while the other prisoner turns informer. The most likely outcome, then, if both men are rational, will be for both of them to inform and therefore both will 'lose', but each loses less than they would have done if they had got the sucker's pay-off by keeping quiet while the other informed.

Source: http://tinyurl.com/6e5qtw

These solutions need traction, and individuals contribute vitally to this. As Wendell Berry noted:

"If change is to come, it will come from the margins… It was the desert, not the temple, that gave us the prophets."

Local community and individual action, informed by cradle to cradle and Nature as Teacher thinking, starts to highlight what we don't want at all – the concept of waste. Local and individual action, influenced by closed loop thinking, becomes a way of articulating what we want more of, say, a better quality of life for all, without destroying social and ecological capital. Questions begin to emerge within local communities on the urgent need for systemic change: for example, 'what about setting a price for carbon emissions, or the mandating of certain building or electricity grid standards, and the removal of subsidies which support environmental degradation?'

But local and individual action can also confirm and reinforce the existing worldview too by leading on guilt and self sacrifice, on regret and the 'ultimate' responsibility of the individual to be less greedy. Did you walk to school? Did you switch the lights off? None of this articulates a sense that we can, as a society, build a sustainable world, by design; merely that we must become better survivors; that what we have no longer works, and that choices are few. These seem dangerous sentiments.

Figure 2.6: Average Income and happiness in the United States, 1957-2002. Credit: D Myers

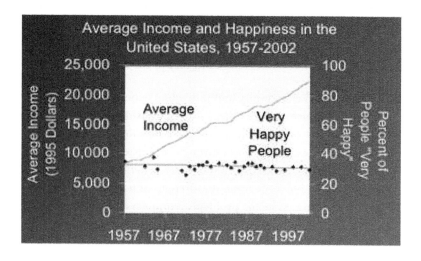

Chapter 2

The Emptiness of Affluence – guilt about Consumption?

This brings us to perhaps the biggest challenge of all. Consumption. Figure 2.6 shows a remarkable relationship. It's a show-stopper in many ways.

As the UK's New Economics Foundation note[8], hardly anyone knows about this, and if they do they don't know how to deal with it, psychologically. All that extra income, expenditure, resource depletion, pollution, loss of life, exploitation, product development and consumption has meant very little if anything in terms of how happy we feel we are. Above an income of around $10,000(US) per year income and satisfaction correlate badly. Below it however is a positive correlation; yes the poor do benefit from more consumption. There is a policy prompt here... as there is in the discovery that societies which are less unequal describe themselves as happier or more content.

But for the developed world, to coin a phrase: 'what was it all for?' It looks like capitalism's promise via economic growth is false beyond that plateau point, but it leaves the question nevertheless of what can be done with a system which promises so much and delivers so little, so inefficiently, for so short a time and which has been built on spreading dissatisfaction with what we own and who we are. When goods saturated the market the system moved onto selling emotional fulfillment through consumption, something for which there would be no end, as there was no hope it could work. This framing has continued to such a degree that the identity more=better is taken as fact. It is simply untrue.

The dread connection, when it comes to learning is that as one choice seems to be equally dissatisfying as the next, the power to discriminate between what matters and what does not is atrophied in the confusion of choices. In the noise of advertising and marketing, ideas become sound-bites, become prepacked, incoherent: the citizen is reduced to consumer, suffering the 'illusion of power' that consumer choices can bring satisfaction or, for that matter, a green and sustainable world.

This is an exciting context for discussion in schools and colleges in that understanding consumerism and its limits is surely at the heart of what we think terms like 'well being' and the 'quality of life' mean, and thus what education for sustainable development might entail. It is very challenging too. As Andrew Szasz notes in *Shopping our way to Safety*,[10] we have turned inward and gone from protecting the environment –

Figure 2.7: 'Work, buy, consume, die'. Credit: Erkka Piirainen
The evidence is growing that even a profusion of choices tends to disable, more choices tends to create less satisfaction[9].

demanding change of politicians and institutions in our role as citizens to protecting ourselves, the individual consumer, by shopping for hazard reduction. But protecting ourselves is not sustainability. It's absurd, it's the blindness to context again.

For some, this hollowness at the heart of the developed world has led to the notion of sustainability as an aspect of a broader rejection of overly materialistic values, individualism and a relocation in strong sense of community, locality and self sufficiency. They are sometimes called New Realists(see box).

New Realists

"This is the search for authenticity, the championing of real food, culture, politics ...and entertainment by a demographic which author David Boyle [Authenticity: Brands, Fakes, Spin and the Lust for Real Life] refers to as the 'New Realists'. This group is easily recognisable — they want to know where their food comes from and what is in it; they want politicians to be honest about the lies they tell and for musicians to play rather than mime; they want to speak to a person rather than a machine when they call a helpline; they seek out local produce and frequent farmers' markets as a means of revitalising community agriculture and bypassing supermarket monopolies.

The New Realists, however, also want to use the Internet and credit cards; many have a soft spot for electronically made dance music; most would like to keep hold of their cars, if only in the absence of decent public transport, and many find that monopolised supermarket produce is actually tasty and convenient after a hard day's work. The emphasis is on searching for and maintaining authenticity — the real, the local, the genuine, the hand made."

Source: Elanor Taylor, Authenticity and the New Realism

There are vibrant overtones of New Realism in many schools with local food, organics and healthy eating campaigns a manifestation, in part, of an unease about consumerism and its meaningless excesses. Increasingly, however, the rationale of schooling is framed as giving ever better income and even more consumption to its most competitive and successful graduates. Tension then, when sustainability is seemingly anchored in a sort of moralising, self denying, guilt tinged consumer arena. Or worse, that the authentic, local and 'real' is linked with sustainability but is only affordable by the better off, the successfully educated and is in turn seen by them as a further measure of their success as discerning, discriminating consumers able to reduce hazards for 'me and mine' and thus deserving of societal approval.

From the cradle to cradle perspective, one aspect of consumerism thankfully looks rather different, as there is no requirement for less consumption per se or a spontaneous change of heart, since the concept of waste is removed and the economy is based on cyclic harvesting of natural resources using the Nature as Capital approach. However, the pattern of consumption will change profoundly, the end of cheap energy will ensure this, and for many consumption will also fall as prices adjust.

But the issue of consumption is real enough. Consumption is often excessive and, on social grounds alone, probably unsustainable as evidenced by increases in debt, bankruptcy, mental illness, and inequality in most societies. With this comes friction and fragmentation (the latest US crime statistics show that one in a hundred adult Americans are now in jail[11] more than the total number of farmers in the country). Up front it might not so much be a question of natural resources, pollution and waste any more.

Prices and Perverse Subsidies – changing the rules of the game in the wrong direction

Being in a cradle to cradle economy is very different to being in transition to one and according to World Watch Institute[12] the opportunity for such change must be taken within the next couple of decades to avoid severe disruption. Again this transition, if it is to be done by intention, needs people with an understanding of how to influence the levers of change. A job for education. As an example, consider prices and consumption.

Perhaps the basis for all modern interpretations of the sustainability theme is that eventually prices must tell the ecological and social truth. This would mean the end of too cheap oil, too cheap

Figure 2.8: Shopping our way to safety. Credit: University of Minnesota Press

SHOPPING OUR WAY TO SAFETY

How We Changed from Protecting the Environment to Protecting Ourselves

ANDREW SZASZ

food, too cheap labour and the ruinous exploitation of resources such as water, fisheries and forests. This would force in efficiency and probably reduce consumption as well as change patterns of consumption. But unless managed well the losers could still be the poor, as the recent effects of 'food to biofuels' policies have shown.

The notion that there are 'rules of the game' is as essential in a global economy as it is in a greyhound stadium. At present, it feels like the greyhounds are in charge but increasingly, in the face of global warming and resource shortages many business leaders, let alone the citizenry, are asking to know what the future rules will be. Business is practical and does know how to respond to systemic change.

Unhappily, the rules of the game work quite the other way at present, with governments paying huge sums to accelerate environmental and community destruction[13] As an example, the box highlights the issue of what are called perverse subsidies.

Rethinking and Redesigning with the Circular Economy

In this chapter, we have touched upon some of the consequences and shortcomings of linear, reductionist and fragmentary thinking, but also its dominance and how it pervades our lives and societies. We also suggest that a progressive ESD needs to reorientate, in search of clarity, to test ideas against different frameworks – particularly the dominant 'Nature as Unlimited Resource' and the emerging 'Nature as Teacher' frameworks.

William McDonough once asked an audience to look on the existing economic arrangement as though it were a design assignment, after all design is a sign of human intention:

"I would like you to design an industrial system for world culture that: treats nature as its enemy to be evaded or controlled; measures prosperity by how much of this we can cut down, bury, burn or otherwise destroy; measures productivity by how few people are working, progress by the number of smokestacks – if you are especially proud, put your names on them; destroys biological and cultural diversity at every turn with one size fits all solutions; requires thousands of complex regulations to keep people from killing each other too quickly; and while you are at it, produces a few things so highly toxic that it will require thousands of generations to maintain constant vigilance while living in terror. Can you do this for me?"[14]

Unusually and perceptively, McDonough and Braungart reject the idea that we have reached an age of limits, we have instead reached the limits of a failed design approach. It is clear that they feel that the state of the existing industrial system is not in any sense inevitable, a given. Far from it. They say a vision for healthy, sustaining commerce does exist:

"The idea that the natural world is inevitably destroyed by human industry, or that excessive demand for goods and services causes environmental ills, is a simplification. Nature – highly industrious, astonishingly productive, extravagant even – is not efficient but effective. Design based on nature's effectiveness, what we call eco-effective design, can solve rather than alleviate the problems industry creates, allowing both business and nature to be fecund and productive."

We have noted McDonough and Braungart's determined use of analogy and metaphor before. Sustainability as a design assignment, business as a cherry tree. Painting new pictures to establish the changed core metaphors. In the context of industrial systems, they also begin talking of products as *nutrients* and about *metabolisms*:

"Commerce worth applauding applies nature's cycles to the making of things. It generates safe, ecologically intelligent products that, like the cherry tree, provide nourishment for something new after each useful life. From a design perspective, this means creating products that work within cradle-to-cradle life cycles rather than cradle-to-grave ones. It means rather than designing products to be used and thrown away, we begin to imitate nature's highly effective systems and design every product as a nutrient.

What is a nutritious product? It's not simply an all-natural product; it's not a recycled product, either. Instead, it's a product designed to provide nutrients to what we have conceived as the Earth's two discrete metabolisms, the biosphere – the cycles of nature – and the technosphere – the cycles of industry. Lightweight food packaging, for example, can be designed to be a nutritious part of the biological metabolism; if it is made of organic compounds it can be safely returned to the soil to be consumed by microorganisms. Synthetic materials, chemicals, metals and durable goods are part of the technical metabolism; they can be designed to circulate within closed-loop industrial cycles, in effect, providing 'food' for the technosphere."[15]

Figure 2.9: Cherry tree in blossom. William McDonough argues that in a cradle-to-cradle world – a world of natural cycles powered by the sun – growth is good, waste nutritious, and nature's diverse responses to place are the source of inspirational human design

So the old design process is replaced...

'Cradle to cradle' mandates all those job opportunities which help close the loop. This green collar expansion would include new skills and fulfill part of that desire from politicians for a 'skills and knowledge-based' economy. It is not anti-growth but instead asks 'what is it that we want to grow?' As a *narrative*, however, as the basis of being able to explain and contextualise our journey once more, without guilt, it brings back to life again the notion of Progress, based now on celebrating Nature's abundance and our relationship with natural systems. There is no longer a disabling distance between humans and Nature when we explicitly understand and use living systems as both model and source of our prosperity.

As Yorkshire-based business leaders IntefaceFlor note:
"At Interface we seek to become the first sustainable corporation in the world, and, following that, the first restorative company. It means creating the technologies of the futurekinder, gentler technologies that emulate nature's systems. I believe that's where we will find the right model."

These are all aspects of a big picture, for sure. Our argument is that in educating for sustainability we have to want and to be able to go well beyond the small steps, to debate the possibilities of a sustainable world *as if it were around the corner*. With the pincers of peak oil and climate change closing in (see Chapter 3), the need to address the transition to a low carbon world does suggest that a 10-20 year time frame is all we are facing to undertake this journey. Crucially we argue that it is in exploring and debating what might be 'the right model' makes most sense of ESD at this juncture. We agree with Interface, that the most useful model at the moment is the 'nature inspired', 'abundance by design' circular economy.

Education needs to be ahead of the curve to be of most value. Surely education's magic is in unveiling the range of what is possible and discussing how it could be achieved? Small steps mean nothing without the big picture and a sense of how to connect one to the other. It is surely not in pretending that Jevons Paradox, the Prisoners' Dilemma, the Emptiness of Affluence and Perverse Subsidies can be ignored simply because their conclusions are challenging or because designing activities to understand them are

"We don't need more carpool lanes. We need to eliminate fossil fuels from our economy. We don't need more recycling bins. We need to create a closed-loop, biomimetic, neobiological industrial system. We don't need to attend a tree-planting ceremony. We need to become expert at ecosystem management and gardening the planet. We don't need another unscented laundry detergent. We need to ban the vast majority of the toxic chemicals upon which our livestyles currently float and invent a completely non-toxic green chemistry. We don't need lite green fashions. We need a bright green revolution."
Alex Steffen

difficult? We need a bright green revolution, and education will be at its very heart because it is in rethinking our society and economy along new lines that the challenge lies.

The future is uncertain of course, and today's confident assertions are tomorrow's foolishness (we know!). Nevertheless, in our view the basics will incorporate a circular economy of some kind along the lines of Chapter 1. This is simply because *unsustainable* development is a disconnection between eco-limits – the basic rules of living systems – and the economy. The whole basis of an education focussed on sustainability is an enquiry about how to, not *whether to*, match up these disparate elements. And for sure the 3.9 billion year experiment which is living systems on the Earth has more to offer than trying to bend living systems to a linear economy.

But before looking at some of the examples of a cradle to cradle approach in action (Chapter 4) and then at how schools and colleges might react (Chapters 5 and 6), there is, according to Christopher Flavin President of the Worldwatch Institute, a need for 'urgency and vision'. Vision we have begun to discuss. 'Urgency' is the subject of Chapter 3 as pressures for transition to a low carbon economy unfold ever more clearly.

SIGNPOSTS
**CPD exercises for the *Prisoners Dilemma, Jevons' Paradox* and the *Emptiness of Affluence* can be downloaded at www.senseandsustainability.com

Chapter 3

The Twin Pincers.

Everything flows, nothing stands still.
Heraclitus

*As a rule we disbelieve all the facts and theories for which we have
no use.*
William James

Our Energy Slaves

147 energy slaves

working 24/7

Doing mechanical work, human bodies can generate about 100 watts of useful energy. If you add up all the power the better-off use, on average, to light and heat our homes, transport us, etc. and convert it to the human energy equivalent, it's an unimaginable opulence by the standards of all the humans who came before us. It is as if our well-being were measured by the number of energy slaves we have learned to command. The average American has 147 energy slaves working non stop.

Figure 3.1: World population graph

This chapter looks at the changes which are likely to cause a reassessment and reorientation of modern life, and with it education. It also examines the idea of change itself: how our dominant world-view, the linear, mechanistic 'Nature as Unlimited Resource' perspective fails to engage with the 'closed loop' perspective, the existence of feedback, and systemic change; how the current worldview prefers instead to work in a fragmentary, short term linear way. Fritjof Capra called this the 'crisis of modernism'[1].

A number of momentous changes are in prospect or progress at this time. Let's choose four: so called 'peak oil' the maximum possible output of easy to obtain oil; an increasingly numerous and wealthy population co-existing with increased inequality; severe climate change; and a fraying of the web of life – the loss of the earth's biodiversity. They are all connected as symptoms of an unsustainable world – let's focus on two characteristics of this. Firstly, that fossil fuels enabled this modern life, replete with our 'energy slaves' (see box). Secondly, that we are on the steep part of several exponential change curves as a result of this fossil fuel economy.

Put another way the use of 'buried sunshine' for industrial development helped start runaway change elsewhere in the system. This kind of change progressively shortens our opportunity to respond as it goes on–see the *Riddle of the Lily Pond* (see box page 64). We are seeing the effects of positive feedback in connected systems. The 'closed loop' and dynamic systems are pursuing us even here, and we seem to be in denial. Never mind the numbers, look at the slopes in figures 3.1 and 3.2... exponential change in progress.

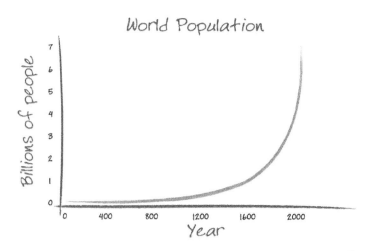

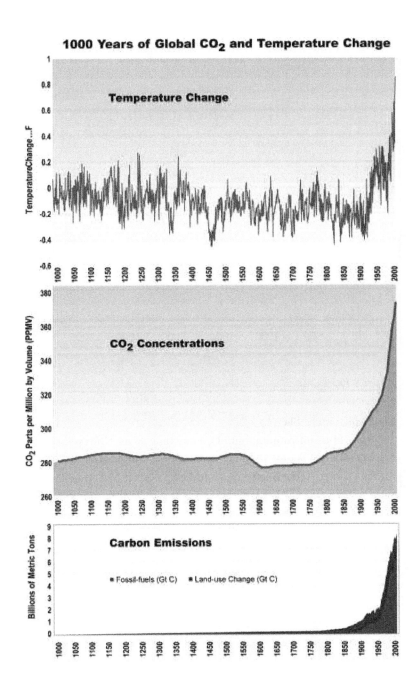

Figure 3.2: 1000 years of global carbon dioxide and temperature change.
Credit:US Global Change Research Programme

Oil Supply - the spead of projections

A 2007 report by the Energy Watch Group, founded by the German parliamentarian Hans-Josef Fell, compared its own oil supply projections to those of the International Energy Agency (IEA).
- 2006: 81 Million barrels of oil/day (Mb/d)
- 2020: 58 Mb/d (IEA:105.1 Mb/d)
- 2030: 39 Mb/d (IEA:116.2 Mb/d)

The difference could hardly be more dramatic.

But first, the new monster under the bed – 'peak oil'. Here is the oil age in a broader context, say three thousand years.

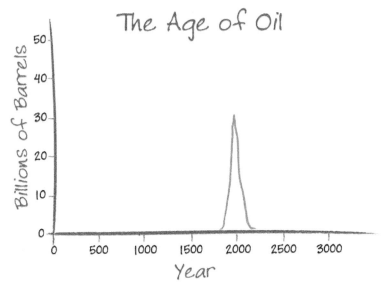

Figure 3.3 The age of oil

The oil spike more like.

The world is not running out of oil any time soon. However, the easy to get oil is reaching the maximum of its possible yearly output sometime soon. According to ex-oil industry commentators such as Colin Cambell and Chris Skrebowski it will peak within the next 5 to 10 years[2]. This matters very much. Figure 3.4 below contains a prediction of world oil demand and production in the 'business as usual' scenario. The Gap is obvious. It's worth remembering that a 5% difference between oil supply and demand quadrupled the price of crude oil in the 1970s oil shock. This impact can be clearly seen on the graphic. The difference now is that there is no easy access to more oil. It also worth noting that a small dislocation gets very large, very rapidly. It's feedback again- a 3% fall in oil production year on year *halves* production within a generation.

There is little debate about whether conventional oil will peak, only about when. The main variables appear to be around how quickly less accessible oil and gas can be found and/or extracted; the results of the 'demand destruction' on the global economy as prices escalate and whether these existing and possible reserves should stay in the ground anyway (because global warming really doesn't need any more stoking up). See Box below for oil extraction impact on biodiversity.

Extracting Canada's tar sands – impacts on biodiversity and local communities

The world's largest untapped oil reserves – in northern Canada – have become the new front line in the battle between environmentalists and the energy industry. Major oil companies are investing billions of dollars in exploiting the Athabasca tar sands. But environmentalists say the tar sands are the world's dirtiest oil deposits and that refining them generates three to four times more carbon dioxide than normal oil extraction.

The accessible oil in the Athabasca tar sands is estimated at 310 billion barrels and gives Canada the world's largest oil reserves – bigger than Saudi Arabia's 264 billion. For Western countries, especially America, Canada's oil is a chance to cut dependence on the Middle East, but the environmental costs could be huge. This is because tar sands comprise viscous bitumen and sand, a mixture that can currently only be extracted by digging it out, destroying the overlying forests and their associated wildlife species.

The Athabasca Region has already been scarred with huge pits, some hundreds of feet deep. Alongside them lie vast ponds that hold the contaminated sands and other residues left after the oil is removed. The River Athabasca and Lake Athabasca into which it flows, are widely believed to be heavily polluted. Medical staff at Fort Chipewyan, on the shores of the lake, have reported an increase in rare cancers in people from nearby communities.

The large oil companies in the area are developing a second extraction method where superheated steam is pumped into the ground to melt the oil so that it can be sucked out as a liquid. However, both processes, and the subsequent refining, require huge amounts of energy – equivalent to up to 30% of the energy contained in the extracted oil. The decision to exploit such oils is provoking a political backlash with Arnold Schwarzenegger, the governor of California, effectively banning them. He has issued a fuel standard demanding a cut in 'carbon intensity', a measure of the carbon dioxide generated in producing and using them. Ten other American states and the European Commission are considering similar measures.
Source: The Sunday Times 20/5/07

Chapter 3

In 2007, the world was producing and using about 85 million barrels of oil per day (Mb/d). Consider the following scenario in which we don't reach peak oil for another decade but feel an 'oil shock' much sooner than that. Let's say we're in the year 2016. Global oil output has risen slowly but steadily from 85 Mb/d to 90 Mb/d. So, it's apparently clear that the 'peak oil alarmists' who predicted in 2006 that oil production would peak sometime in 2006-2008 were wrong. But such a conclusion would miss the real message of peak oil warnings. Oil production is at least slowing, while demand continues to rise — currently at about 2 Mb/d per year. Once the demand curve for oil starts bumping up against the production curve, oil prices will skyrocket, and the economic impacts will be severe.

Figure 3.4: Plenty of oil but at what price and how easily available? Meanwhile oil discoveries lag way behind. Graph credit: Colin Campbell, ASPO Ireland and Scientists for Global Responsibility

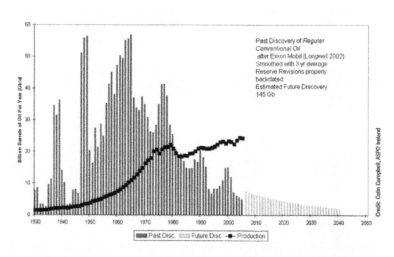

Conventional crude oil – past and future discovery compared with production

The world changes as soon as that fossil fuel supply-demand gap opens up and we are then on a transition to a low carbon world whether we choose it or not. The 'rules of the game' have been changed for us. Because oil and gas has a market price and as yet carbon emissions do not (give or take some emissions trading), the impact of the Gap is immediate and profound.

The obvious connection of oil and gas (gas may last a little longer before peak) with transport, heating and electricity is only part of the picture. So oil dependent have we become that we *eat* oil – up to 10 kilocalories of fossil fuel are needed to provide one kilocalorie of food energy on the plate[3]. For some products such as air freighted lettuce it is ten times that[4].

Figure 3.5: Selection of foods and their input-output energy balance. Credit: Ernst Ulrich von Weizsacker/Immo Lunzer

Selection of Foods and their Input-Output Energy Balance

High values correspond to low energy efficiency. For greenhouse vegetables in winter we expend over 500 calories of foreign energy for one calorie of food.

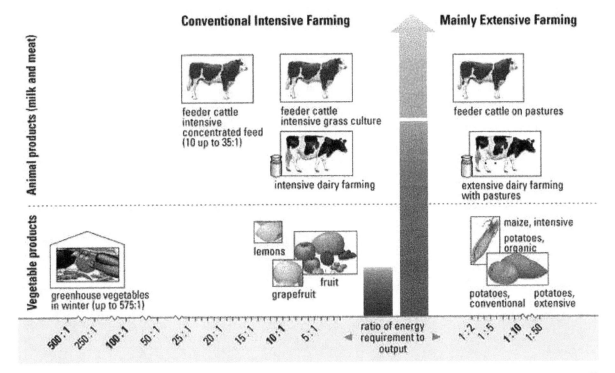

Oil Price Effects

The World Bank quote that for any 10% rise in the price of oil there would be a 3% rise in fertiliser prices. For agriculture as a whole the reaction is 1.7%. Even for metals the response is 1.1%.

Figure 3.6: World oil demand cartoon. Credit: John Ditchburn

In an industrial food system it's not only farm machinery and fertiliser and pesticide production that depends on oil and gas – the food processing, distribution and supermarket focussed shopping habits of the developed world are built on oil as well. Talking of shopping: plastics are an obvious oil based product, a core product of the packaging industry as well a myriad of products in themselves.

But oil is more pervasive than even food, transport, heating and power. We wear oil. Half the clothing produced is based on synthetic oil based fibres, and the biggest clothing source outside of this – cotton – is the most heavily treated with pesticides and herbicides. More oil. We live oil: cement and brick making is fossil fuel intensive; many houses have no means of heating other than oil and gas or electricity – nor even chimneys.

Suburbia is a mode of living designed around the car, and cheap oil. The film The End of Suburbia[5], although somewhat shrill, maps its vulnerabilty to high oil prices. The very idea of suburbia being just a phase of human habitation rather than a permanent feature seems faintly outrageous, but as Chapter 4 outlines, plans for some new cities, even in an oil state like Abu Dhabi, are not on the suburban model – they are walkable and public transit dominated.

Biofuels

Transition to closed loop models of development is quite a challenge but it is particularly ironic that an attempt to close the fossil fuel Gap, to put off the day, is being made via biofuels (or 'agrofuels'). In the USA this largely consists of using corn production to make ethanol for transport fuel rather than food. Producing this corn will be at great cost in terms of fossil fuel energy inputs and *subsidies* – now running at $11 billion a year worldwide. The real cost will be even greater when the propects of food shortages and food riots in poorer countries is factored in. The conversion of natural forests to palm oil and sugarcane plantations to make biofuels is another major cost. Such large scale biofuel manufacture suits big agriculture, the auto and fossil fuel industries, the biotech industry and governments, and for this reason change has been rapid.

Rising populations are a problem especially in India and China, whose burgeoning middle classes are predictably switching their demands from cereals and grains towards meat and fish as income goes up. As recently as 2000, the FAO was confident there was enough food production in the pipeline to meet expected demand. After all, the Green Revolution was a great success at one level: new varieties of staple crops, irrigation and increased fertiliser use increased grain production 2.5 times between 1950 and 1984. But, faced with rising oil prices, rapid climate change, changing diets, the loss of irrigated land, climbing rates of pollution from farm animal slurry, pesticide and fertiliser run off, crop yields are now falling[6]. This looks like a vulnerable linear production process. It hardly need be said that in a competition between the use of land for crops to make biofuels and profitable livestock rearing for middle income people, compared to basic foods, it is the poor who will lose out first and most dramatically. With it comes the possibility of more failed states and intense migratory pressures, amid death and misery. It's a lot to sacrifice for a failed framework of thinking.

"The Queensland Oil Vulnerability Taskforce (Australia) concludes that the overwhelming evidence is that world oil production will peak within the next 10 years."
Andrew McNamara, Minister for Sustainability, Climate Change and Innovation, Queensland's Vulnerability to Rising Oil Prices 2007

'Fuel made from food is a dumb idea to put it succinctly,' says Ronald Steenblik, research director at the International Institute for Sustainable Development's Global Subsidies Initiative.

Delivery van being fuelled up with biodiesel

Waste=Food – biofuel production from waste vegetable oil

Unlike much current large-scale biofuel production (see main text), the use of waste vegetable oil for biofuel has real potential to contribute to the development of circular local economies in both rural and urban settings[7]. Just one example: Growing with Grace, an organic nursery and market garden in the Yorkshire Dales is a member of the Clapham community co-operative which has set up a scheme to convert waste vegetable oil into fuel for diesel engine vehicles. The market garden uses the biodiesel to 'feed' their vans delivering organic fruit and vegetables around the area. The biodiesel manufacturing plant at the market garden gives members of the cooperative scheme the opportunity to run their vehicles off the waste vegetable oil that is brought from a nearby business. The cooperative also plans to use vegetable oil collected locally from fish-and-chip shops, hotels and restaurants, preferably within a 20 kilometre radius of Clapham.

The refining process involves a number of stages, including heating, filtering, adding calculated solutions, chemical testing and removing final water particles through filtering methods. It is classed as carbon neutral because each burned litre of the biodiesel has already been offset by the amount of carbon dioxide absorbed by the plant material as it was growing. As well as producing biodiesel from the vegetable oil, the manufacturing process also produces glycerol and potash as by-products. These are added to the compost made in the garden waste composting facility at the market garden (the compost is then ploughed into the soil to grow salads and a range of other vegetable crops).

Source: Clapham Community Cooperative/Growing with Grace, 2008

In addition to the issues surrounding peak oil are those around climate change. The vicissitudes of climate change are well understood, in outline at least, following report after report from the *International Panel on Climate Change* (IPCC), the *Stern Review*, Live Earth (July 2007) and the release of the films *11th Hour* and the Oscar winning *An Inconvenient Truth*.

The work of the IPCC demonstrates that most scientists are now in agreement that we are experiencing accelerated climate change. It is clear that every year serious corrective measures are delayed climate change becomes more and more expensive to deal with. The *Stern Review* in 2006 made this plain. Act now to hold carbon dioxide levels in the atmosphere at around 450 parts per million (ppm) and it will cost 1% of global GDP but at 550ppm it will cost 20% of global GDP. It's another exponential relationship. Unhappily, the IPCC report of November 2007 concluded that the carbon dioxide equivalent level of 450ppm had already been reached[8]: 10 years ahead of predictions.

That is bad news. Another worry is that as carbon dioxide levels rise in the atmosphere the climate may tip over into a turbulent state with irreversible consequences. In James Lovelock's *Revenge of Gaia* a few humans remain, clinging onto the edges of the Arctic in an otherwise devastated, overheated world.

This notion of a 'tipping point' is yet another idea from an iterated, systems view of the way the world works. Change is often sudden in iterated systems – systems with feedback loops – not incremental. All exponential curves tend towards sudden collapse. Understanding this better seems a rather obvious first step in reconnecting ourselves.

Riddle of the Lily Pond

What Exponential Change looks Like and Why it Matters

A French riddle. In this riddle, a lily pond has a potentially virulent lily that apparently will double in size each day. If the lily grows unchecked it will cover the entire pond in 30 days, choking off all other forms of life in the water by the time it covers the entire pond. If a sceptic waited until 50% of the pond was covered before taking any remedial action to save the pond, when would he or she act? The answer: on the 29th day of the month. But by then, it would be too late.

The world can debate when corrective action to address climate change needs to begin, but if it is exponential growth we are seeing then waiting until the proverbial 29th day is a mistake of the first order.

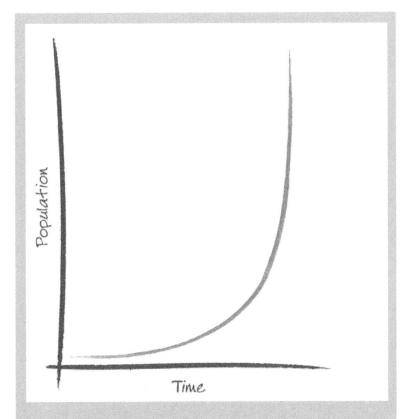

Figure 3.7: Population growth over time

How long does it take to double? Exponential growth explained

A percentage change in something each year always blows up in the long run much faster than linear increase.

The formula is

Doubling time (td)= .693/growth

So if growth is 10% (0.10) a year then the original figure will double in .693/.1 = 6.93 or approximately 7 years

On graphs, such trends look a lot like this. There are quite a few of them in this book.

"Scientists have begun to realise that change could be sudden, not gradual-in some cases it could happen within a few decades."
Professor Joachim Schellnhuber, climate scientist

Pressure for change reaches a critical level and suddenly the system changes its characteristics, never to return to the past, at least not in any imaginable future (see box for the 12 Tipping Points of climate science). Systems science also tells us that the nature of feedback is very complex and the causes of the change of state may be hidden and arrive 'out of the blue'. Systems scientists recognise that humans are not in charge, change isn't linear in complex systems and change and connection are fundamental, whilst parts are not.

It all seems reasonable, so where do we teach this magic world of the non-linear system; of how it is the normal state of the world, and the linear and mechanistic the exception or the more limited case? It might be a litmus test of how far changed thinking is really changed.

Sensitive Places...12 Tipping Points

In 2004, the then Research Director at the Tyndall Centre for Climate Change Research Joachim Schellnhuber identified 12 global natural systems that may be prone to tipping point phenomenona. Schellnhuber argues that if any one of these 12 systems is pressurised to tipping point it could initiate sudden, catastrophic changes across the planet[9].

1. Amazon Rainforest
2. North Atlantic Current
3. Greenland Ice Sheet
4. Ozone Hole
5. Antarctic Circumpolar Current
6. Sahara Desert
7. Tibetan Plateau
8. Asian Monsoon
9. Methane Clathrates
10. Salinity Valves
11. El Nino
12. West Antarctic Ice Sheet

Source: Mother Jones November/December 2006 Issue
The Thirteenth Tipping Point By Julia Whitty http://tinyurl.com/ygwjby

Chapter 3

Applying a framework based approach to the question of nuclear power?

Discussion of nuclear power is never far away in any energy debate. It's especially relevant in the face of climate change and peak oil. Miquel Torres put it this way:

"The question of whether nuclear power can provide a big part of the worlds' energy needs is extremely important in the Peak Oil debate, because it is the only alternative energy source, beside coal, providing the type of electricity production necessary for the current electric grid model: big, base-load capable power plants. If that role is fulfilled, the current electricity production system can continue beyond Peak Oil, and even expand to provide the energy necessary for electrified transport. If it falls short, a new energy model is needed."

The approach we have suggested in this book is to try and identify if the product or service is provided within a linear or closed loop model and whether it is non-toxic.

A further criterion is that prices 'should tell the truth' – reflect overall costs, including environmental and social costs in the longer term.

The nuclear industry does not look very sustainable. Supplies of ore appear limited: "the analysis of data on uranium resources leads to the assessment that discovered reserves are not sufficient to guarantee the uranium supply for more than thirty years."[10] The existing process is linear – although fast breeder reactors are slated for around 2030. The waste from power stations is toxic to a very high degree. The nuclear industry worldwide is heavily subsidised, especially in research and development, decommissioning costs, security, infrastructure and limited liability.

The understanding that a cradle to grave model with price distortions is unsustainable provides somewhat different avenues for framing subsequent discussion. It becomes more likely to focus on how nuclear might fare as a stopgap, or the reasons why politics might outweigh longer term considerations. Or indeed, whether, with fast breeder reactors, a closed technical nutrient cycle could be established.

Figure 3.8: Human perspectives on geographical space. After Simmons and Company International

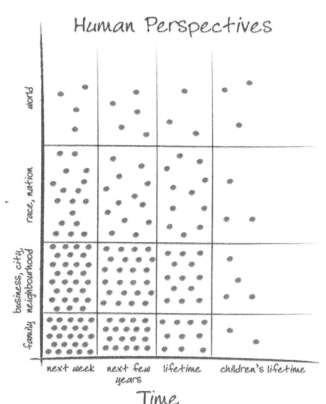

The Twin Pincers and the role of education

So in the face of the twin pincers of peak oil and climate change and the enveloping 'crisis of modernism', a new framework for thinking is needed. It is highly appropriate that schools and colleges aim to discuss ways to break out from the hypnosis of business as usual.

It has always been one role of education to extend thinking from 'me and mine' to events, and then to ideas, from 'now' to encompass historical trends and future possibilities. Never was the need more urgent – yet this is a very difficult arena for educators to work in. Nowadays, we know that a sense of disconnection is pervasive among many people, seemingly whatever the information available. There are several aspects to it.

Here is an example of the difficulties facing colleagues who may wish to address these bigger picture issues – represented graphically.

A demographic sample was asked to record the frequency of their thoughts in different categories of space and time.

The graph demonstrates we are clearly creatures of the here and now. Perhaps it was always the case.

There are now more profound changes in society too, causing frequency of thinking to rise within the lower left of this graph. The rise of the consumer and individualism has meant that ideas of progress or society, or indeed the very notion of the value of ideas themselves, have tended to diminish sharply. For many people, ideas have been replaced by an easy cynicism, ironic attitudes and a focus on personal feelings and fulfillment. And although many young people do not fit this profile it is a significant trend. The Me Generation slipped into 'Generations X and Y'(see Box).

Reality bites-A Generation X film

"Troy was in a band. Troy did sweet FA. Troy said things like, 'There's no point to any of this. It's all just a random lottery of meaningless tragedy and a series of near escapes.' So I take pleasure in the details. You know – a quarter-pounder with cheese, the sky about 10 minutes before it starts to rain, the moment where your laughter becomes a cackle. And I sit back and I smoke my Camel Straights and I ride my own melt."

"We didn't believe in global communism, but that doesn't make us advocates of global capitalism. We may not believe in God or institutions but that's missing the point; because we don't believe in the absence of God or institutions either. We don't even believe in immutable knowledge. We prefer Wikipedia – a limitless, editable source that's as fallible as its contributors".

Source: Generation X: The slackers who changed the world by Patrick Neate[11]

Since everything goes then nothing really matters. It's not just at the individual level that this is happening. Politics too has largely abandoned Ideas and is run as a consumer orientated pick and mix against a background that says that democracy can be best expressed through individuals and their choices in the market place.

These are not accidental or temporary trends. According to the seminal BBC TV series *The Century of Self*,[12] they are part of the response to the need to maintain social control in an era of affluence. These trends also generated a solution to the overproduction of goods and quieted resistance to growing inequality and environmental problems (see box).

These characteristics of modernity are as much a matter for sustainability and education as climate science or the price of oil: after all we must connect before we can do anything about the prospects for transition to a low carbon world. However, ours is a culture of disconnection, of magpie eclecticism, of uncertainty and it seems, a society of comfort junkies! This is summed up by Patrick Neate :

"Both New Labour, under Tony Blair, and the Democrats, led by Bill Clinton, used the focus group to regain power. They set out to mould their policies to people's inner desires and feelings, just as capitalism had learnt to do with products."
Adam Curtis, The Century of Self

"For all our one-time dread of yuppie aspiration, we have grown comfortable with its fruits. We don't eat sushi because it says something about us, we eat it because we like it. We don't wear Calvin Klein underwear to make a statement, but because it's what we damn well wear. We don't even drive SUVs around our crowded cities because of some misplaced one-upmanship, but because they're genuinely frightfully convenient if you've got two small kids. And we'll let nothing disturb this convenience. (other)... tendencies will never get in the way of our mod cons and our pluralism will never outgun our desire for comfort. It is the one thing about which we're never relative. And this scares even me."[11 ibid]

The Consumer and the Illusion of Power

Out of the conformity and mass consumerism of the post- second world war era arose the idea that what prevented people from leading satisfying lives was the obligation and duty imposed by elites in society, and that this 'policeman inside our heads' had to be deposed. It is the Sixties. Self development, self expression was what mattered. This troubled corporations as it also contained an anti-materialistic and anti-corporate element. What if people stopped shopping? Public relations and marketing businesses had long worked to understand the irrational drives and feelings of people in order to sell products on the (false) basis that they could meet emotional needs. What these analysts now noticed was the spread of the idea of self development and self fulfilment as a key concern of individuals. Between 1970 and the early 1980s the desire for self fulfilment spread from about 2% to 80% of the population.

To meet these changes, corporations recognised that products and services would need to be more individualised, which in turn would reinforce the idea that an individual could and should be making these choices as part of their emancipation. Society was atomising and reconfiguring not in an idealistic manner but as lifestyle groups. Manufacturing and new technologies changed to match and reinforce this trend and went further, marrying the consumer to brands and the shopping experience (boutiques, malls etc) as an innoculation against consumer fatigue. So the counterculture of the 1960s became the new consumer culture.

The new idea was that people could be happy simply within themselves and that changing society was irrelevant – so politics changed too, as people voted more as consumers, and the mantra of 'choice' spread ever more widely into public services like health and education. However, these choices, for the majority, are decided by powerful interests and what is presented always reinforces these interests. Most 'choices' in our consumer society represent 'an illusion of power'.

It comes as no surprise in such a consumer and individually focussed society to see the proposal that individuals can be left-as with everything else-to 'make the difference' when it comes to dealing with the environmental and social consequences of economic expansion. But they can't. Just as you can't shop your way to happiness, you can't shop your way to sustainability. It is also an illusion of power.

It is scary. This disconnection is both a caricature and real, as this excerpt from the *Mother Jones* article *The 13th Tipping Point*[13] makes clear:

"A 2005 study by Anthony Leiserowitz, published in Risk Analysis, found that while most Americans are moderately concerned about global warming, the majority — 68% — believe the greatest threats are to people far away or to nonhuman nature. Only 13% perceive any real risk to themselves, their families, or their communities. As Leiserowitz points out, this perception is critical, since Americans constitute only 5% of the global population yet produce nearly 25% of the global carbon dioxide emissions. As long as this dangerous and delusional misconception prevails, the chances of preventing one or more of Schellnhuber's 12 points from tipping (see box page 66) are virtually nil."

It is impossible to wish away this sense of disconnection and apathy, characterised, for some, in just one word: 'Whatever' – the impatient dismissal of others, their ideas and values. Not least because it is a predictable end point of a marketing of self and products in a universe of atoms, individuals and (only) stuff. The modern day celebrity is a wonderful illustration. They are usually famous for being famous. It is not a celebration of talent, genius or contribution (which takes commitment) but the instant propulsion of the seemingly ordinary to recognition which is so often being celebrated. 'And it could be me' is the thought behind it all.

Given its pervasiveness, addressing this sense of disconnection is not a tack-on task for schools and colleges – it will have to reflect more profound changes in society. However, a part of any reconnection will be in showing the practical rewards of connection as well as changing the philosophy, the outlook. A transition to a low carbon economy, surprisingly, might contain levers for both.

"Those in power would now control the self not by repressing it but feeding its infinite desires."
Adam Curtis

The hidden roots of the word 'apathy'.
"The word derives from the Greek apatheia, meaning non-suffering. Given its etymology, apathy is the inability or refusal to acknowledge suffering."

TRANSITION TOWN
TOTNES

Figure 3.9: Transition town Totnes logo

Transition to a Low Carbon Economy as a rebirth of Community

If it is oil and other fossil fuels which have fed unsustainability by widening the gap between ourselves and the products and services we use – and the people who provide them – its rapid contraction, logically, will provide the possibility of a simultaneous reconnection between people and planet, economy and ecology and between community and individual. But to succeed, any reconnection needs to be managed well, and within a coherent rationale (framework for thinking). It is this prospect which is so encouraging in the rapid development of what calls itself the Transition Towns movement.

This is a community reaction aimed at mapping and facilitating transition while protecting local resources and communities. It is a positive response to peak oil which has great resonance, as shown by its rapid growth. It has resonance because it puts under the umbrella of peak oil hitherto often disparate groups who now look convincingly like innovators for a wider society in changed circumstances. It's close to home, practical, and informed. It uses the internet as a very effective tool. Moreover, it seems like a coming home for many in its loose membership. As Richard Heinberg, one of the leaders of the peak oil theorists writes:

"We have only a dwindling amount of time to build ...the needed alternative infrastructure. It has been clear for at least 30 years what characteristics this should have — organic, small-scale, local, convivial, cooperative, slower paced, human-oriented rather than machine-oriented, agrarian, diverse, democratic, culturally rich, and ecologically sustainable."[14]

Another thread in this long list, for anyone who wishes to investigate the main texts and practices associated with transition towns, is the importance of a 'living systems' perspective. It's there in organic farming , in permaculture, in 'ecologically sustainable', in slow knowledge (see box) and slow food tracts. It would be surprising if it was not.

Transition towns make most sense as a part of a changing worldview – the localisation/get-involved – again transition towns argument shares the circular economy notions of the Dongtan city designers in China and companies such as General Electric, Toyota and

InterfaceFlor (see chapter 4). Although they are a different expression of closed loop, circular economy thinking, what characterises both is the energy or passion, a sense of recovering purpose i.e. the *possibilities* of reconnection.

ESD work on initiatives like transition towns allows an exploration with learners about ideas such as disconnection, disconnected communities and reconnection. We can use transition towns to develop careful thinking about ideas and frameworks before moving to informed action. Discussion on transition towns can bring to life terms such as ' local well being', 'participation' and 'social inclusion' and begin to develop a broad and shared understanding of living systems and the challenge of the circular economy.

It is obvious that schools and colleges are not immune from the broader changes detailed in this chapter (we discuss this more in Chapter 6). The transition to a low carbon world is world changing and it will be the messages in the prices – the economics – which will catalyze rapid change when it happens.

From special pleading (as environmental and social issues are sometimes described), to central meanings, and at the heart of these meanings might be a systemic framework for thinking. Perhaps learners need to understand that linear thinking itself is partly predicated on fossil fuels, which enabled and reinforced ideas of take–make–and–dispose. Instead, we hope that the debate will collect around what Schellnhuber insists is 'a re-invention of modern society' and behind that what we have called in shorthand the 'cradle to cradle' or closed loop model. Thus the systemic framework for thinking shifts too – from linear to closed loop.

Schools and colleges may wish to shift the focus of learning programmes to address these emerging agendas: from mechanistic to systems worldview; from conventional big business to 'closed loop' business models and the circular economy; from 'fix it up', to clean production; from managing by target to managing by means. In making connections with grassroots movements such as transition initiatives, systems thinking emerges in the ideas of local food and low input organic farming, devolved energy and community resilience. It can therefore share the enthusiasm of the New Realist agenda.

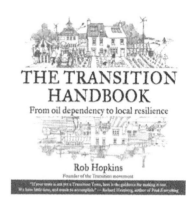

Figure 3.10: Transition towns book cover

Slow Knowledge
The difference between fast knowledge and slow knowledge could not be more striking. Fast knowledge is focused on solving problems usually by one technological fix or another; slow knowledge has to do with avoiding problems in the first place. Fast knowledge deals with discrete problems whereas slow knowledge deals with context patterns and connections... Fast knowledge is mostly linear; slow knowledge is complex and ecological.

Source: David Orr The Nature of Design: Ecology, Culture, and Human Intention

In the next chapter we look at some of the leading examples of 'cradle to cradle' thinking here in the Yorkshire and Humber region and elsewhere.

SIGNPOSTS

**Keep Cool.* A board game on climate change choices devised by the Potsdam Institute[15]

Chapter 4

Innovative business in a sustainable low carbon future.

You never change things by fighting against the existing reality.
To change something, build a new model that makes the old model obsolete.
Buckminster Fuller

If the machine inspired the industrial age, the image of the living system may
inspire a genuine postindustrial age.
Peter Senge et al., in Sloan Management Review

Business is the only mechanism on the planet today powerful enough to
produce the changes necessary to reverse global environmental and social degradation.
Paul Hawken

All of these statements contain a claim to a part of the truth about a transition to a sustainable low carbon world. All coincide in a 'cradle to cradle' or circular economy. Better world, new metaphors, led by business. As William McDonough notes: "the goal is a safe, healthy, just world, clean air, soil and power, that is elegantly enjoyed."

In educational contexts it is about applying a Nature as Teacher perspective to all aspects of industrial society – as a way of critiquing with learners what exists now, and as a way of framing the possibilities of a sustainable future. It is a kind of 'eco-literacy' but explicitly understood as a coherent approach consistent with our evolving understanding of science (especially non-linear systems) and the realities of a globalised economy. In this way, our ESD programmes can provide a narrative which makes sense to everyday aspirations. It does not necessarily make sustainability easy though.

When learners ask the questions 'What can I do?' and 'What's in it for me?' and they come from the same quarter it changes the game. Now, it becomes a matter of joining in for something rather than fighting against. In our view, the emerging circular economy is something coherent enough for students to get a handle on, and to question or extend – no story is ever complete.

Education has always claimed a role in creating 'informed citizens.' But it has also always been pragmatically interested in how change in the way dominant institutions work affects the prospects for its students. In short, how business and the economy evolves influences education policy and schools and colleges (no doubt reflected in what parents and students demand). New 'green collar' jobs, income and careers in the circular economy will make these changes compelling, something that conventionally framed 'environmental' or 'social' concerns never did.

The leading edge of a shift away from the machine inspired industrial age is now visible across the world. With it come the demand for new skills, creativity and competencies based on insights from living systems. New jargon too: biomimicry; natural capitalism; design for disassembly; feebates; zero waste ... There is a real sense of business on the move, for its own purposes and working successfully with aspects of this living systems model. These are exciting developments and in this chapter we consider some of the leading business organizations working with this agenda – their work is inspirational and provides a wealth of opportunities for the design and development of new ESD programmes. Let's start with cities....

Ecocities: Masdar, Abu Dhabi and Dongtan, China

The city of Masdar in Abu Dhabi will be a zero carbon, zero waste community, one that will be entirely car free. Actually, it will be the first in the world, if things go according to plan. The design team and architects leading at Masdar are Adrian Smith and Gordon Gill Architecture. Within the walls of the city will be a new university, Future Energy Company's HQ, an Innovation Center, and special economic zones. The mixed-use, high-density city aims to be a centre for new ideas on producing energy. With narrow walkways and shaded streets, occupants will be able to access transportation nodes with relative ease. And because the city is tight sans sprawl, the surrounding land will be used for wind and solar farms and research fields. And why would an oil state be interested in these things...??

Meanwhile, in China, the global design and engineering company Arup has been contracted by the Shanghai Industrial Investment Corporation to design and masterplan the city of Dongtan. The first phase of Dongtan aims to be completed by 2010 and will accommodate a population of up to 5,000. Later phases of development will see the city grow to hold a population of around 80,000 by 2020 and up to 500,000 by 2050.

The delicate nature of the Dongtan wetlands adjacent to the site has been one of the driving factors of the city's design. The plan is to protect and enhance the existing wetlands by returning agricultural land to a wetland state creating a 'buffer-zone' between the city and

Figure 4.1: The Masdar Headquarters. This will be the first mixed-use positive energy building in the world for the world's first zero-carbon, zero-waste, car-free city called Masdar. As a 'positive energy' building, the design aims to generate more energy each day than it consumes. Credit: Adrian Smith and Gordon Gill Architecture.

the mudflats. The project will increase biodiversity on Chongming Island, and will create a city that runs entirely on renewable energy for its buildings, its infrastructure and its transport needs. Dongtan will recover, recycle and reuse 90% of all waste in the city, with the eventual aim of becoming a zero waste city. Dongtan eco-city incorporates many traditional Chinese design features and combines them with a sustainable approach to modern living.

Figure 4.2: Dongtan, near Shanghai, China. Credit: Arup

Some of the sustainability features in Dongtan[1]:
- all housing will be within seven minutes walk of public transport and easy access to social infrastructure such as hospitals, schools and work
- although some may choose to commute to Shanghai for work, there will be employment for the majority of people who live in Dongtan across all social and economic demographics
- Dongtan will produce sufficient electricity and heat for its own use, entirely from renewable sources. Within the city, there will be practically no emissions from vehicles – vehicles will be battery or fuel-cell powered.
- farmland within the Dongtan site will use organic farming methods to grow food for the inhabitants of the city, where nutrients and soil conditioning will be used together with processed city waste.
- the development of techniques that increase the organic production of vegetable crops will mean that no more farmland will be required than is available within the boundaries of the site.

Chapter 4

First big cities then big business...

InterfaceFLOR is a worldwide leader in the manufacture of modular flooring and part of Interface Inc. headquartered in Atlanta. InterfaceFLOR in Europe is based in Halifax, West Yorkshire. Interface offers floorcoverings for the commercial and residential markets. Interface is trying to break away from the old-fashioned, wasteful 'linear' industrial process and move toward a more natural 'cyclical' or 'closed loop' pattern which uses or recycles any waste produced (waste=food), rather than just disposing of it. Interface takes back its products at the end of their useful life and uses natural forms of energy, such as wind and sunlight, to power their factories.

Ray Anderson, the founder and Chairman of Interface Inc, and the visionary behind the change in culture within the business, known as Mission Zero writes:

> "We can look to nature for the inspiration, the guiding principles to make the changes needed in the industrial system to make it as effective as nature is – waste free, resource-effective and resource-efficient, benign, operating on sunlight the way nature operates on sunlight; taking nothing and doing no harm."

Interface want to go beyond doing no harm, they want to be restorative and have modelled the shift from the typical 20th century business to the prototypical business of the 21st century – based on 'cradle to cradle' thinking.

It's a long route: carpet and flooring is traditionally a resource and energy hungry business. They are determined to climb what they call the Mount Sustainability.

In the diagram below of the Interface model[2] note the similarity with William McDonough's technical and biological nutrient cycles which we discussed in Chapter 2.

Note also that the fully developed model depends on redesigning commerce. Interface recognizes that, on its own, it cannot become this company. This is the same as individuals acting locally but also demanding a change in the rules. There can be no sustainability without systemic change, individual companies can only point the way.

> *"There is no 'away.' Nothing is destroyed (first law of thermodynamics). It will disperse (second law of thermodynamics). Forget 'away' there is no such place to throw anything. Stopping pollution upstream is what we must do, leaving the toxic stuff in the lithosphere* where the process of evolution put it to make way for us. It must be left there*
> **InterfaceFLOR**

*Lithosphere: the rigid outer layers of the earth's crust and mantle

Figure 4.3: InterfaceFLOR factory, Halifax, England. Credit: InterfaceFLOR

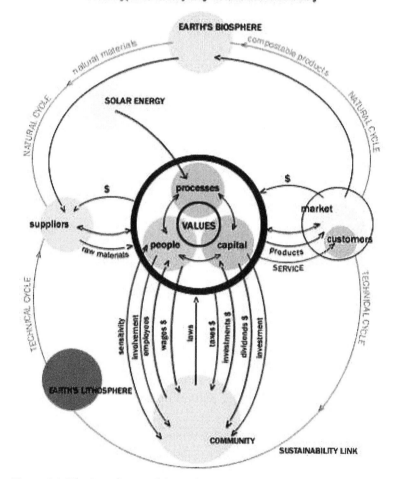

THE INTERFACE MODEL
Prototypical Company of the 21st Century

EARTH'S BIOSPHERE

natural materials

compostable products

NATURAL CYCLE

NATURAL CYCLE

SOLAR ENERGY

$

$

processes

market

suppliers

VALUES

customers

people

capital

raw materials

Products

SERVICE

TECHNICAL CYCLE

TECHNICAL CYCLE

sensitivity

involvement

employees

wages $

laws

taxes $

investments $

dividends $

investment

EARTH'S LITHOSPHERE

COMMUNITY

SUSTAINABILITY LINK

Figure 4.4: The Interface model. Credit: Interface Inc.

Here is Interface on that point:

"Dream a little: maybe even the tax laws eventually will shift taxes from good things, such as income and capital (things we want to encourage), to bad things such as pollution, waste, and carbon dioxide emissions (things we want to discourage). What if perversity could once and for all be purged from the tax code? When the price of oil reflects its true cost, we intend to be ready. That would truly change the world as we have known it, especially the world of commerce."

Business and systemic change at regional level

The need for systemic change to address the low carbon economy is recognised by Yorkshire Forward, the regional development agency in Yorkshire&Humber Region, England. In a pioneering initiative, the regional development agency is working with the 100 largest regional business organisations to cut the region's carbon emissions (25% cut by 2016).

A regional low carbon economy has been defined as: "a regional economy where, in response to binding targets, managed programmes of carbon emissions reduction are embedded in organisational practices across the private and public sectors. Organisations will have identified and taken responsibility for the full life cycle, supply-chain, direct and indirect costs of their carbon emissions."

Programmes of work will include a focus on low carbon technologies and sustainable consumption and production. However, to achieve a low carbon economy, it is recognised the approach must also be integrated into all regional policies and strategies including housing, transport and regeneration. Yorkshire Forward has established The Sustainable Futures Company, to drive forward programmes to put the region at the centre of the emerging low carbon economy. Yorkshire Forward will:

- lead the top regional businesses and public agencies – towards a lower carbon economy, focusing on energy, innovation in low carbon technologies, good business practice and land management
- demonstrate how to decouple economic development from increasing energy and resource use in individual businesses and the wider economy, moving towards a One Planet Economy
- work to an established carbon budget which reflects national and regional climate change priorities
- identify skills shortages and support education and training programmes that help to build capacity of businesses working on renewable and other low carbon technologies

Source: Low carbon economy policy. Yorkshire Forward, 2008

Model cities, model firms, yes but the context matters. It always does. Some sense of the principles of a sustainable economy is crucial. Interface has been influenced by and influenced organisations such as *The Natural Step* and by the work of Amory and Hunter Lovins and Paul Hawken in particular. It was in the 1999 book *Natural Capitalism*[3] that a modern business model of a pathway to a sustainable economy first came to widespread notice.

It is a practical real world approach which accepts, as Interface does, that this transition is not easy or immediate. It starts with resource efficiency but as we discussed in Chapter 2 it does not end there. It is labelled radical resource efficiency too – it's not a few percent here and there – and it is not enough on its own. Clearly Interface are already radically increasing resource efficiency. But what next?

Lessons from Nature – A bigger list
- Waste=Food (Waste=food is just a start, a way of pointing towards a different mode of thinking)
- Self-assemble, from the ground up
- Evolve solutions, don't plan them
- Relentlessly adjust to the here & now
- Cooperate AND compete, not just one or the other
- Diversify to fill every niche
- Gather energy & materials efficiently
- Optimize the system rather than maximizing components
- The whole is greater than the sum of its parts
- Use minimal energy & materials
- 'Don't foul your nest'
- Organize fractally
- Chemical reactions should be in water at normal temperature & pressure

Source: list collected by Jeremy Faludi. See his essay Biomimicry For Green Design (A How-To) for explanation http://tinyurl.com/4nrn7s

'Radically increased resource efficiency' is the first principle of Natural Capitalism. It offers not only increased profits, but also the solution to many of the environmental dilemmas facing the world

today. It greatly slows depletion of resources at one end of the economic process, and the discharge of pollution (resources out of place)
at the other end. It creates profits from not having to pay for esca-
lating levels of resource inputs. And radical resource efficiency also
buys time, forestalling the threatened collapse of natural systems.

That time should then be used to implement the other three principles of Natural Capitalism. These are:

- Eliminate the concept of waste by *redesigning the economy on biological lines that close the loops of materials flows* (emphasis added). We
  have discussed this in some detail in Chapter 2 and the key ideas of
  this zero waste approach are shown visually in figure 4.5.
- Reverse the planetary destruction now underway with programmes
  of restoration that invest in natural capital. (forest, freshwater, wetland, marine ecosystems etc)
- Shift the structure of the economy from *focusing on the processing of
  materials and the making of things to the creation of service and flow*
  (emphasis added); so as to reward resource productivity and loop-
  closing;

Figure 4.5: The circular economy

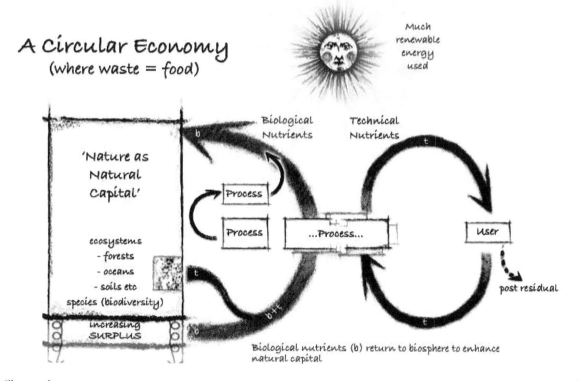

A Circular Economy
(where waste = food)

Much renewable energy used

'Nature as Natural Capital'

Biological Nutrients

Technical Nutrients

Process

Process

...Process...

User

ecosystems
- forests
- oceans
- soils etc
species (biodiversity)

post residual

increasing SURPLUS

Biological nutrients (b) return to biosphere to enhance
natural capital

Nature as Capital

Ecosystems can be seen as Capital assets. Depending upon how they are managed, they supply a stream of benefits, without which human life would cease to exist. These benefits include goods (such as seafood and timber), processes (including water purification, flood control, and pollination), life-enhancing attributes (such as beauty and serenity), and the preservation of options (genetic diversity for biotechnology). These benefits flow as long as the ecosystem is carefully nurtured and kept intact. Like a business, living from Income and reinvesting in the Capital makes sense. A business eating its capital is on the way out. "Once people see ecosystems as capital assets, a light bulb goes on,"
Gretchen Daily, Stanford University Adapted from Natural Capital Project. http://tinyurl.com5ajzp3

Services not Goods

The emphasis on Services rather than Goods is another central idea of the new circular economy. Beginning in the mid-1980s, Swiss industry analyst Walter Stahel[4] and German chemist Michael Braungart independently proposed a new industrial model that is now gradually taking shape. Rather than an economy in which goods are made and sold, these visionaries imagined a service economy wherein consumers obtain services by leasing or renting goods rather than buying them outright (their plan should not be confused with the conventional definition of a service economy, in which burger-flippers outnumber steelworkers). Manufacturers cease thinking of themselves as sellers of products and become, instead, deliverers of service, provided by long-lasting, upgradeable durables. Their goal is selling results rather than equipment, performance and satisfaction rather than motors, fans, plastics, or condensers.

The system can be demonstrated by a familiar example. Instead of purchasing a washing machine, consumers could lease it, paying a monthly fee based on how much they used their washing machine. The washer would have a counter on it, just like an office photo-copier, and would be maintained by the manufacturer on a regular basis, much the way mainframe computers are. If the machine ceased to provide its specific service, the manufacturer would be responsible for replacing or repairing it at no charge to the cus-tomer, because the washing machine would remain the property of the manufacturer. The concept could likewise be applied to com-puters, cars, DVD players, video decks, refrigerators, and almost every other durable that people now buy, use up, and ultimately throw away. Because products would be returned to the manufac-turer for continuous repair, reuse, and remanufacturing, Walter Stahel called the process 'cradle-to-cradle.'

Model cities, model businesses, model products – the impor-tance of biomimicry

Biomimicry, the conscious emulation of life's genius, is a profound approach to making manufacturing sustainable. Janine Benyus, author of the ground-breaking book *Biomimicry*, asks the simple question 'how would nature do business?' She points out that nature delivers a wide array of products and services, but very differently from the way humans do. Nature, for example, runs on sunlight, not high flows of fossil fuels. It manufactures everything at room temperature, next to something that is alive. It creates no waste, using the output of all processes as the input to some other process. The discipline of biomimicry takes nature's best ideas as teacher and then imitates these designs and process to solve human problems. Many leading businesses – from DuPont, General Electric, Nike, and Interface – use the principles of biomimicry to drive innovation, and design superior products.

Biomimicry and carpets

Ray Anderson, founder and Chairman of the billion dollar a year carpet company Interface, tells the story of the creation of his carpet tile product Entropy. David Oakey, head of product design at Interface, sent his design team into the forest with the instruction to find out how nature would design floor covering! 'And don't come back', he instructed, 'with leaf designs – that's not what I mean. Come back with nature's design principles.'

So the team spent a day in the forest, studying the forest floor and streambeds until they finally realised that it is total chaos there: no two things are like, no two sticks, no two stones, no two anything..... yet there is a pleasant orderliness in this chaos.

They returned to the studio and designed a carpet tile such that no two tiles have the same face design. All are similar but all are different. Interface introduced the product into the marketplace as Entropy, and in 18 months the design was top of their bestseller list.

Entropy carpet. Credit: InterfaceFLOR.

The advantages of Entropy were astonishing: almost no waste and off quality in production. The designers could not find defects in the deliberate imperfection of having no two tiles alike. Installers can put the carpet in quickly without having to take time to get the pile net all running uniformly. They could take tiles from the box as they came and lay them randomly, the more random the better – like a floor of leaves. Moreover, dye lots now merged indistinguishably which means sellers do not have to maintain an inventory of individual dye lots waiting to be used.

Entropy is made with recycled content in a climate neutral factory; 82 of Interface's products are now designed on the principle of no two alike. These represent 52% of Interface's sales. Using principles like waste minimisation and biomimicry has enabled Interface to bring the company's carbon dioxide emissions to roughly 10% of their 1996 levels.

Source: State of the World 2008, Worldwatch Institute

This 'service not goods' approach is an example of 'thinking like a mature forest', where an ever more diverse and complex ecosystem develops within a fairly fixed flow of energy and nutrients.

A further intriguing ecosystems parallel is between the economy of the oil age and a Post-oil transition economy. The oil age economy could be represented by the early stages of succession in a forest, where a few aggressive fast growing species dominate. A post-oil economy is represented by the climax stages of ecological succession where a more diverse collection of plant and animal species thrive together in the mature forest.

These forest and economy parallels are becoming ever more explicit and the insights being derived very sophisticated. An example is the book *What we Learnt in the Rainforest – Business Lessons from Nature*[5] by former Mitsubishi Chief Executive Tachi Kiuchi. To quote him:

"Companies are living systems. They flourish according to the very same principles that foster sustainability in nature."

In a similar vein, one of the featured businesses in Peter Senge's book, *Profit beyond Measure*[6] is Toyota, soon to be the biggest car

Chapter 4

manufacturer in the world. Their management is world renowned for efficiency. They are also famous for their eco-poster child, the Prius car and their successful efforts to green their operations. But perhaps of far more relevance here is the modelling of their management approach on living systems. Described as 'management by means' – as opposed to the familiar management by results. Peter Senge writes:

"business leaders can acheve higher and more secure levels of profitability if they organise work according to the systemic principles infusing nature and cease to drive work with quantitative goals."

Exactly how the Toyoto management approach manifests itself is beyond the scope of this book[7] but the moral is clear: if the likes of Toyota are happy and prosperous using a living systems under-standing then this shift in emphasis is firmly in the mainstream, not some idealistic academic dalliance, and further evidence of the under-mining of the dominance of the 'mechanical' worldview.

There is a strong sense of optimism and change here, but the world is far from this in reality. Toyota obviously also sell the Landcruiser as well as the Prius and make handsome profits for shareholders. The reality, it is said, is more hype than hope. A raincheck may be necessary...

Greenwash: the realities of business?

"You can't put a lettuce in the window of a butcher's shop and declare that you are now 'turning vegetarian'."
John Grant The Green Marketing Manifesto.

That's Grant's clever and amusing illustration of greenwash, the deflection of criticism or the painting of a firm to be greener than it deserves through tokenism. The emergence of an ecological world view is occuring in an economy whose short termism and sheer unsustainability is breathtaking and almost overwhelming. A classic example of greenwash is the kerfuffle over plastic bags, a symbolic and high profile battleground. As Tony Juniper, executive director of Friends of the Earth, points out: "until the big supermarkets reduce the amount of energy used in their stores, minimise the distance that food travels and review their relationship with farmers, saving a few plastic bags is just window dressing."

Services Not Goods – The Freedom Bike

The 'freedom bike' Credit: Austinevan

Paris's Vélib', or 'freedom bike' scheme, has turned the city cycling mad. You simply pick up a bike from one of the ubiquitous stands, ride it along for your short trip and drop it back at any random stand at your destination. The first half-hour's pedal-time is free, with charges rising steeply afterwards. This is not the first scheme to provide bikes for cheap short-hires – Amsterdam, Copenhagen and Oslo got there first, and Lyon was the pioneer in France – but Paris aims to be the biggest. More than 1.6m hires took place in the first month from the 800 bike stands. The unisex bikes are pro-vided by the poster advertising company JCDecaux to Paris city hall in return for ad space in the city, so at no cost to the taxpayer. The Green party has congratulated Parisians for leaping on a scheme that shows that protecting the environment 'is not a punishment, but a delight'.
Source: The Guardian 16/8/07

The supermarkets know this but marketing brand image has long been seen as important or more important than mere product to large firms. To see greenwash deployed to this end with increasing subtlety and persistence does not make the proponents of the circular economy either naïve or unduly idealistic about business attitudes and practices. The challenge is on the other side: in the face of a transition to a low carbon economy in the near future what alternative to a circular economy does one have in mind? The real economy of pricey carbon, phosphorus, copper, and nitrate molecules (to name but a few) hollows out the greenwash illusion and critical thinking in education accelerates this process. At some time business will engage fully – and dealing with plastic bags might just have been a useful exercise. The main question for educators, just as it is for community meetings in transition towns, or more widely, is: "how can we make sense of a low-carbon economy? So... what next? What are our choices?"

In its Yearbook of 2008 UNEP's analysis, is that the world is experiencing new invention and imagination "on a scale perhaps not witnessed since the industrial revolution of more than two centuries ago." This is more than a happy coincidence[8]. And it is quite some assertion. The coming of the green economy will not primarily be because there is a change of heart but because the constraints and opportunities for business are changing and because we are discovering more effective models. It will be because the careerists eventually see advantage in hitching themselves to it. And there is no shame in anticipating this. We need to give them a helping hand.

Developing World. Opportunities at the Bottom of the Pyramid.
"Learning to close the environmental loop at the Base of the Pyramid is one of the fundamental strategic challenges — and opportunities — facing multinational corporations in the years ahead".

The Base Of The Pyramid Protocol[9]: Toward Next Generation BOP Strategy p5

The base of the world economic pyramid (BOP) is the 4 billion people in the world whose annual per capita income is less than $1,500, the minimum considered necessary to sustain a decent life. For well over a billion people, roughly one-sixth of humanity, per capita income is less than $1 per day. Figure 4.6 shows the pyramid complete.

Exhibit 1: **The World Economic Pyramid**

Annual Per Capita Income*	Tiers	Population in Millions
More Than $20,000	1	75–100
$1,500–$20,000	2 & 3	1,500–1,750
Less Than $1,500	4	4,000

* Based on purchasing power parity in U.S.$
Source: U.N. World Development Reports

This extreme inequity of wealth distribution reinforces the view that the poor cannot participate in the global market economy, even though they constitute the majority of the population. In fact, given its vast size, this tier represents a multitrillion-dollar market. However, to attempt to re-create resource intensive and wasteful types of consumption patterns in this tier would be disastrous. The challenges for BOP development include many of those mentioned thus far – in thinking more of services than goods. For example: pest control service teams rather than selling spray cans; call by call use of a mobile phone; of waste=food packaging for small individual servings; of localisation and deep dialogue with communities. It can be seen as a source of innovation in systems and technologies, a chance to leapfrog the wastebound North. However, the reality is complex and this following case study of selling into the emerging Tier 2 and 3 market illustrates just how.

Figure 4.6: The world economic pyramid. Credit: UN World Development Reports

Clever Little Car

Tata Motors has unveiled the world's cheapest motor car at India's biggest car show in the capital, Delhi (January 2008). The vehicle, called the Tata Nano, will sell for One Lakh (100,000) rupees or about US $2,500 (£1,277) and enable many in developing countries to move from two to four wheels. The four-door five-seater car, which goes on sale later this year, has a 33bhp, 624cc, engine at the rear. It has no air conditioning, no electric windows and no power steering, but two deluxe models will be on offer. Tata will initially make about 250,000 Nanos and expects eventual annual demand of one million cars.

Figure 4.7: the Tata Nano car Credit:Sujathafan

Company chairman Ratan Tata said the launch of the Nano was a landmark in the history of transportation. He said the car was "a safe, affordable and all weather transport – a people's car, designed to meet all safety standards and emissions laws and accessible to all".[10]

As India and China expand their economies rapidly so their people's aspirations grow too. 300 million Chinese have escaped from grinding poverty in the last two decades. So what can we say on the spread of mobile phones or large urban conurbations, or the preference for meat and dairy in an otherwise limited diet? Or about the likes of the Tata Nano? There have been criticisms by environmentalists in India and unease in the West.

- Environmentalists worry that a car so cheap could lead millions down what they see as the wrong road, with soaring car ownership damaging the environment and locking India into greater dependence on oil. India imports 70 percent of its crude oil.
- Indian climate change expert R K Pachauri, chairman of the Intergovernmental Panel on Climate Change, says the One Lakh Car is giving him 'nightmares'.
- Anumita Roychoudhury, of the Centre for Science and Environment in New Delhi, said "it's just not sustainable, whether from an environmental point of view or in terms of congestion."

In the UK a car like the Tata Nano would be called 'environmentally friendly' based on its small size and good fuel economy. But while the efficiency revolution may let us drive on half the gas, the productivity revolution – the Nano is the cheapest car ever made in real terms – may make it affordable to twice as many, or more. The Nano is deeply problematical for our global economy. Its Jevons' Paradox again. As Jeff Vail, the US energy analyst notes[11]:

"The danger of an economy that seems adept at squeezing ever more productivity out of each hour of labor and barrel of oil is that this same trend that could help the West soften the impact of Peak Oil seems poised to make the global energy supply crunch worse by making energy consuming cars affordable to an ever greater portion of the world's population. An expanding consumer base makes it much more difficult to achieve overall gains via efficiency: if the number of cars doubles, the efficiency must also; if the number of cars triples, is it realistic to triple miles per gallon across our global fleet? Quadruple?"

Chapter 4

The Tata Nano – what is the problem?

A surge in car ownership is underway across Asia anyway...

But is the Nano 'too cheap'? Can we morally even suggest limiting access to cars to a growing middle class? Wasn't efficiency and productivity supposed to be a good thing for the environment and society? Will rising oil prices ration these and all vehicles – will the better off be able to hang on to their privileged access to road space? Should they?

India and China (among many states) subsidise fuel so that rising prices do not have such a rationing effect... What are the alternatives? What about sustainability, or the future of transportation where carbon is fully costed? Where does the Nano car fit?

Ivan Ilich, in *Energy and Equity*, said "participatory democracy demands low-energy technology, and free people must travel the road to productive social relations at the speed of a bicycle." Whatever happened to such grassroots visions of development?

From Toyota to the Wakefield Sewage works. From Cardboard to Caviar. A case study of integrated 'closed loop' thinking on a medium scale

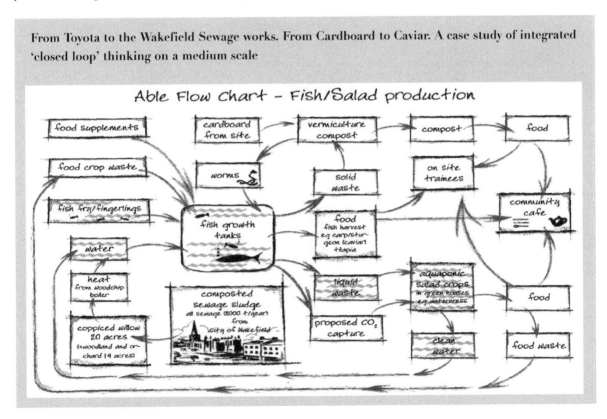

'Cardboard to caviar' fish farm

An interesting fish farming social enterprise has emerged in the city of Wakefield, England. Designed and developed by the Green Business Network it is a lovely example of a 'closed-loop business'. Waste (cardboard) from one process is turned into feedstock for another process – to feed worms which are then fed to sturgeon, carp and catfish on the fish farm – the loop is 'closed' when the fish are eaten by humans. The working principle for the business is 'waste=food'!

This fish farm uses renewable energy firing its boiler to heat the fish tanks. The boiler uses willow wood chip which is grown nearby and fertilised using all the composted sewage from the city of Wakefield (8000 tonnes/year). The fish farm also provides transitional employment and training opportunities for disadvantaged young people. Groups of less academic and disengaged youngsters travel to do project work on the Wakefield site. Practical tasks and skills such as path-laying and food-growing are succeeding in engaging such groups. The scheme is an environmentally aware and socially-inclusive business, aiming to produce fish for specialist and ethnic minority communities, including recent asylum-seekers and economic migrant groups often ignored re provision of their traditional cultural food types, e.g. sturgeon (caviar), carp, tilapia, catfish, etc. The Yorkshire&Humber ESD Teacher Trainers Network is currently working with the fish farm on the development of circular economy teaching resources for use in initial teacher training courses at regional universities.

Source: Cardboard to Caviar fish farm Green Business Network (2008)
http://www.theableproject.blogspot.com/

The conclusions for education are clear – shouldn't we be an enthusiastic part of this? There could be valuable insights here for how schools and colleges are managed (see Chapter 6).

Two questions in particular, follow in the context of education for sustainability and both need to be addressed. Firstly, is this starting point, this narrative, important enough to occupy something like a guiding role in education for sustainability?

We believe the answer is a provisional yes. If George Lakoff is right about frameworks (that some framework is always operating and we can't make sense without invoking one or more) then using the deep frameworks which make up a systems worldview should not be problematical. Such a framework is a tool after all. It is a powerful and widespread perspective which informs ecological processes, non-linear science, leading business practice and, lest we forget, accepted notions of participative learning itself! It seems to tick all the boxes. It is a fine place from which to survey the horizon.

There are other frameworks, (see 'Five Ways to Fit' box on p36) but for us, the debate is about how to make better sense of sustainability and, as a frameworks debate, the ecological worldview has a justified place on the front bench.

Or, if Lakoff is wrong, then it's back to every situation is different and there is no grand narrative (post modernism) or the idea of universal rationality – objective investigative learning processes. Or maybe something else entirely...

The second question for ESD is how might the core of all this engage with learners? This is something which we explore in more detail in Chapter 5. What is needed most, if Lakoff is right, is the opportunity for learners to try out, to absorb or 'click into' another set of metaphors, this other worldview. This is something Stephen Sterling has been developing with his pioneering and extensive systems thinking work–the *linkingthinking* project in Scotland[12]. The lessons needed here are those which promote a changed sense of how the world works. The Center for Ecoliteracy, a well respected US non-governmental organization, puts it this way:

"When systems thinking is applied to the study of the multiple relationships that interlink the members of the Earth Household, a few basic principles can be recognized. They may be called principles of ecology, principles of sustainability, or principles of community; or you might even call them the basic facts of life. We need a curriculum that teaches our children these fundamental facts of life:

- *that an ecosystem generates no waste, one species' waste being another species' food;*
- *that matter cycles continually through the web of life;*
- *that the energy driving these ecological cycles flows from the sun;*
- *that diversity assures resilience;*
- *that life, from its beginning more than three billion years ago, did not take over the planet by combat but by cooperation, partnership, and networking.*

Teaching this ecological knowledge, which is also ancient wisdom, will be the most important role of education in the next century."

Forest energy flow and nutrient cycles—developing insights on how Nature works

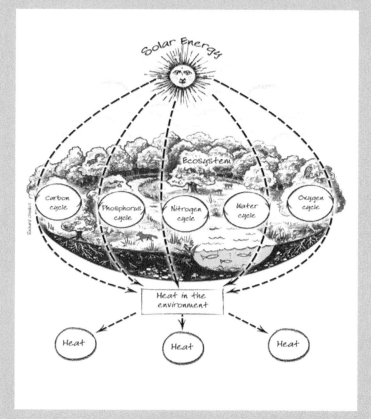

Forest energy flow and nutrient cycles

Life on Earth depends on the circulation of certain key chemicals and the one way through flow of energy in ecosystems such as this forest. Dotted lines in this diagram show energy flow, solid lines chemical cycling . Note that above ground many species (biodiversity) connect in complex food webs eg oak trees, insects, spiders, voles, owls, weasels, deer etc. Within the forest soil are even more complex species-rich food webs – fungi, bacteria, earthworms, etc

For all practical purposes, the total amount of matter on the earth is fixed. Our planet is a closed system with no matter entering or leaving. The chemicals necessary for life must thus be continuously cycled and recycled through the ecosystem. Water and the chemical elements such as oxygen, carbon, nitrogen and phosphorus are constantly circulated within these nutrients cycles. The Sun's energy is of course used to drive and maintain the cycles. Note that while matter is cycled and recycled, energy is not – there is a one-way through flow of energy through the Biosphere. One of the major problems with our present take-make-dump society is that it is a linear system based on a one-way movement of both matter and energy. This wasteful system needs to end. Instead, we need to develop insights on how ecosystems such as this forest works and then explicitly design society's products and industrial processes to mimic the cyclical processes found in Nature.

Adapted from: Charles Krebs, Ecology–the Experimental Analysis of Distribution and Abundance, Harper (1978) and Energy Flow through Ecosystems, Unit 1-3 Producers and consumers, Open University (1974).

All this ecological understanding documented by the Center for Ecoliteracy is essential – although we'd suggest that in Nature competition *and* cooperation are present.

Sense and Sustainability suggests that we need to reinforce this ecological learning by explicitly, consciously, building a bridge from a sense of Nature and how it works *into the late modern world*. Into this populous urban technological world: how do we make this city sustainable for example (figure 4.8)?

Figure 4.8: Shanghai, China at night. Credit: Gareth Jones.

So it is not an argument for a pre industrial, hand made society, it is not some ruralist dream.

As we have shown in this chapter, this bridge building is beginning to happen amongst leading large and small business organizations, designers, planners and architects. And in a serious way, as this surprising quote from IKEA shows:

"No one has been promoted to the senior management level who does not have a strong commitment to these issues. Before we engaged in sustainability, there were managers who did not take environmental and social issues to heart. These managers are no longer at IKEA. We take great care to get the right people promoted."

Thomas Bergmark, Social Responsibility Manager IKEA

Ecomagination and General Electric

General Electric has developed a company wide environmental initiative called Ecomagination, a business initiative to help meet customers' demand for more energy-efficient, less emissive products and to drive reliable growth for GE. Ecomagination also reflects GE's commitment to invest in a future that creates innovative solutions to environmental challenges and delivers valuable products and services to customers while generating profitable growth for the company.

The plan calls for increased spending to develop new technologies such as wind-power generation, diesel-electric hybrid locomotives, more-efficient aircraft engines and appliances, and advanced water-treatment systems.

The company pledges to spend $1.5 billion a year on such research by 2010, more than double the $700 million it spent in 2005. GE also aims to double the revenue goal over that period for products that provide better environmental performance, to $25 billion a year, and expects more than half of its product revenue to come from such products by 2015.

In September 2008 GE and Google announced a joint renewable energy technologies partnership.

Source: General Electric. Pers.comm. April 2008. World Business Council for Sustainable Development, September 2008.

But this bridge building is not done very often within education. In schools and colleges Nature is, quite rightly in many respects, for studying of itself, for ecology, biology and botany and appreciating or celebrating. Nature is not often treated as design or business studies teacher – and the idea of Nature as Capital is rarely addressed. Nature is seldom viewed as the source and the origin of our social and economic sub systems – the sustainable resource base of the economy. It is like the school pond, too often intellectually and practically fenced off, literally a distance from the classroom. Interesting, but not often relevant. This will not work for long. We need to remove the distance between humans and Nature.

We support the notion that to close the gap between Nature and society and economy will require many of the strengths of environmental education in its appreciation and knowledge of Nature, its practical investigation and even humility, or spiritual response to Nature. But to bridge the gap will require far more: as educators, we have to debate how the insights of Nature can be best applied explicitly to a modern world in transition to a low carbon economy and to the processes of innovative teaching and learning itself–which is also based on participation and feedback. With a systems perspective, there should no longer be a gap, the 'Teacher is respected and the learner cared for' as the Taoists might put it. Mutual dependency instead of antagonism.

In the next chapter we introduce some classroom examples that illuminate these transferable lessons of natural systems.

SIGNPOSTS

**The Circular Economy Ball Game* A game simulation for a large group using plastic balls, laughter and a broom or two. Download at www.senseandsustainability.com

**Norman Foster: Building the Green Agenda* http://www.ted.com/talks/view/id/174

Chapter 5

Learning and Transition

The teacher is respected and the student cared for.
Tao De Ching

In education we have argued that pressures for change come from two principal directions. A key priority is the need for a resilience, a broader set of skills, rooted in the practical needs of a population faced with the real cost of hydrocarbons. To be creative, innovative, socially skilled, adaptable, practicably knowledgeable about food, cooking, health, local energy, networking and design... The list is longer than this but it is the practical and vocational side of a low carbon, 'green collar' economy. Some of the work currently carried out under Education for Sustainable Development could be set in this context (probably framed as adapting positively to a changing world rather than 'saving the planet'). Much more, by way of community building is suggested in the transition towns handbook[1].

We argue that the second urgent priority for ESD is that of a changed framework for thinking, shifting the dominant metaphors towards a more enabling 'cradle to cradle' living systems perspective. We have talked about the core metaphors being consistent and thus *reinforcing*:

*This is how Nature works
*This is how physical science, economics, psychology, etc increasingly sees change
*This is how innovative business sees it

.....and what about educational practice?

When schooling is about the transmission of knowledge and some skills in chunks which are tested for a standard quality then this still looks like school as a production line. But good schools and colleges have always been more than this – at least over the last 30 years. Determined efforts to introduce active and participatory learning, to attempt the education of the whole person, have offered a counterpoint to the traditional instrumental approach to education.

Basic participatory learning cycle
based on Honey and Mumford

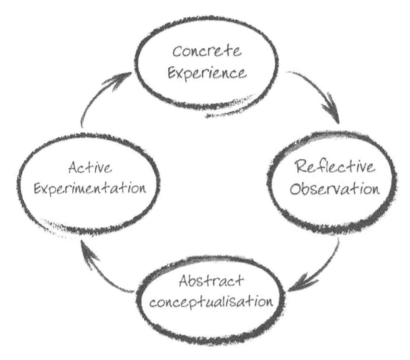

Figure 5.1: Active learning cycle

The diagram above summarises a familiar active learning cycle. It demonstrates a good iterative model: it uses feedback and the outcomes are therefore uncertain – but not necessarily chaotic. Feedback is necessary for learning – systems without feedback fail. Teacher and learner are in a dance, a dialogue with each other and the context. A student is a participant, not an object to be completed or a machine part to be engineered. It's all pretty familiar and has an intuitive appeal – depending on perspective.

John Miller[3] has developed a useful summary of the relationship between different worldviews and teaching and learning approaches and aims (see box on the next page).

Learning

John Cleveland, Joann Neuroth & Stephanie Marshal have developed a schema of nonlinear organizational learning [2]: Nonlinear means that there is not a proportion between input and output. A small input can give enormous results and vice versa. Individual and organizational learning is nonlinear because it is cyclical with the outputs of one cycle becoming the inputs of the next cycle.

* *The learners are provided with a rich variety of inputs;*
* *Different learners follow different paths;*
* *The outcomes are emergent and cannot be foretold;*
* *Learning is self-organized by the learner's activity in designing it;*
* *Disciplines are integrated and roles are flexible;*
* *There are rapid iterations between the parts & wholes;*
* *People coevolve together in a learning community.*

An idealized systems thinking approach, or just a recogition of how people tend to learn and how complex it is?

Worldviews and learning

worldview	theory of change	curriculum and instruction position
fragmentalism	*traditional/conservative*	*transmission*
humankind is divorced from nature and can therefore exploit the environment; nature is made up of a series of building blocks; individuals are encouraged to compete in the market place as free agents	traditions must be maintained - change needs to be checked and controlled; parts of a system can be changed if they do not work effectively; social change comes about through the efforts of successful individuals	education is a one-way top down-ward movement of certain knowledge, skills and values; its focus is the traditional school subjects taught in a traditional way; the student is seen as a passive recipient of conveniently packaged and programmed blocks of teaching
pragmatism [modern scientific]	*intervention*	*transaction*
humankind can improve the environment through the use of rational planning; science and techology can solve the problems the planet faces; individual behaviour is predictable and can be monitored through legislation	change needs to be introduced and managed in a rational and scientific manner; social improvement requires deliberate intervention by some individuals for the good of others	education is a dialogue between the student and the curriculum; the focus is on teaching strategies which facilitate problem solving; the student is seen as rational and capable of solving problems if given the right tools
holism [systems thinking]	*organicism*	*transformation*
all life on the planet is interconnected and interdependent; meaning is derived from understanding relationships; individuals cannot act in isolation -the actions of any one impact on the system	change is an inevitable and natural function of a system; change only has meaning in the context of the system; social improvement comes through dismantling the human made barriers to change	education is a process of personal and social development; it focusses on the aesthetic, moral, physical and spiritual needs of the student as well as her cognitive attainment; the student is viewed as a whole person

Source: John Miller, The holistic curriculum, Ontario, OISE Press (1988) and in Greenprints for Changing Schools, S.Greig, D.Selby and G.Pike, WWF/Kogan Page (1989)

Imagine an active learning pedagogy joined with the other dynamic 'closed loop' systems seen in nature and innovative business. A powerful synergy then seems possible as it's the same core imagery: *how nature works and science sees the world, the basis of teaching and learning and the expression of a sustainable economy.*

From this:

1. Develop learners insights on how Nature works

2. Develop learners insights on how innovative 'cradle to cradle' industry works

3. Develop learners insights about 1 and 2 using innovative participatory learning approaches

To this:

1, 2 and 3 share the same systems thinking – using 'closed loops' and 'feedback'

Figure 5.2: Closing the loops

In the *Sense and Sustainability* poster (and in Chapter 7) we use the idea of a winning line at a fruit machine: all the bunches of cherries in a row. Very satisfying. Caveats abound but we are talking about sense and sustainability, about grasping a *sense* of the big picture and with it a rationale for change. It makes 'sense' not as a way of managing the decline of the existing, inefficient, ineffective and unjust arrangement by turning down the wick on the burning of fossil fuels. Rather, it makes 'sense' as a coherent, useful, synergistic approach to transition to a low carbon world which can be a better, more satisfying place to live. Moreover, we are convinced that as an intuitive and resonant frame of thinking it will eventually remove the need to have something labelled an education for sustainability (or ESD) at all. The thinking will be just a part of how we educate, much as the linear and fragmentary ethos prevails now.

Prompting shifts in the core perceptions

An obvious place to start, and one beloved of the Centre for Eco-literacy for example is the primary school food garden. It is not so much prompting shifts as making the learning explicit, as the young learner's world view is more integrated at this age.

Haworth Primary School, Yorkshire

Children at Haworth Primary School harvest pumpkins

The children of Haworth Primary School in Yorkshire have a healthy appetite for the fresh homegrown vegetables on their plates at school. The 40 pupils of the school's twice-weekly after-school Gardening Clubs plant and tend the vegetables, but the whole school is involved in harvesting the vegetables, shelling peas and peeling potatoes in the kitchen and then eating 'their vegetables' for dinner.

In the spring term of 2003, the club started growing vegetables in raised beds that make planting and weeding easy for the children. They entered the produce into the local flower and vegetable show. Initially, it was the wider community that benefited directly from the fresh vegetables they grew. They still do. The children carry boxes of vegetables over to the old people's home where the residents enjoy meeting the children and getting the home grown produce.

In 2005, the children started to see their produce on the plates at lunchtime. Since then, peas, tomatoes, lettuce, cucumber, peppers, runner beans, carrots, leeks, potatoes, Brussels sprouts, cabbage and beetroot from the garden have all been served up for lunch. There is enough produce during the growing season to have set days when the school eats home-grown produce as part of their school meals. Following requests from the children, a small orchard with apple, cherry, plum and pear trees has already been planted.

The teachers of Haworth School make full use of the gardens in teaching the curriculum, helping the children to develop good numeracy skills by weighing pumpkins and measuring sunflowers. Recently they held a carrot tasting, comparing two organically grown varieties from the garden with supermarket carrots, which scored badly in the comparison.

The rewards are great. The teachers report that the behaviour and concentration of the pupils has improved markedly since they started to eat what they grow. Steve Thorpe, the school gardener says: "over the years I have had lots of children with various behavioural problems, or special needs. The gardening has given them something to focus on and have ownership of. It has changed their whole attitude towards school life and given them a much calmer approach to the way they deal with day to day situations."

Source: Soil Association School Food Awards 2006. In 2008 Haworth Primary School was selected to be a Food for Life Partnership Flagship School and Community and as such they are working on various aspects of food leadership, food quality and provenance, food education, and food culture

Practical work in the school food garden provides good opportunities to learn about: the existence of conditions for plant growth, interdependence of healthy plants and soil and the insects and bacteria; energy flow from the sun; the circular flow of nutrients in living systems. The core idea for us to visualise with our learners is that of connection, flow, cycles, and that waste=food (see supplementary activities online). With our learners we need to demonstrate that this is how it works in nature (such as forests, see diagram on page 94). If nature is to be our teacher, we need to explicitly design and discuss our school food gardens (and our farms!) from the basis of connection, flow, cycles and that waste=food.

Applying this core idea to other contexts of increasing complexity would be a familiar form of progression. Here are a few other illustrative examples.

Take the tree in the forest: sunshine is its energy source; it benefits from those around it; it has local sources for water and nutrients; it is a productive habitat for the maintenance of biodiversity; it is a home and a food source; its waste is food for other species and its presence changes the flow of wind and temperature. As part of a huge forest, the tree even affects climate. Could housing be more like trees in forests?

Circular flows can be discovered in their absence when looking at suburban housing for example. Here is the typical house and its connections—electricity, water and sewerage, heating, transport. It is striking how 'linear' it is. Take, use and dispose.....

Figure 5.3: Cut away of suburban house

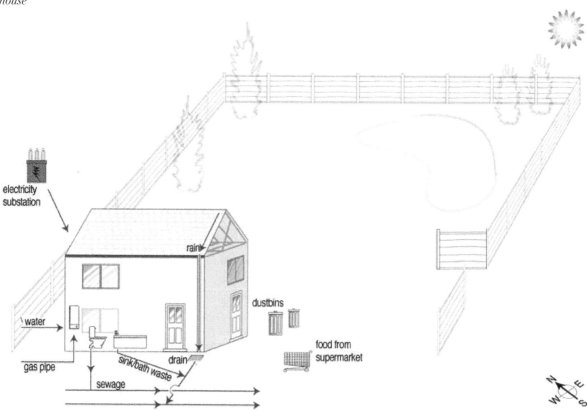

Chapter 5

Substituting more 'closed loops' is an interesting exercise.

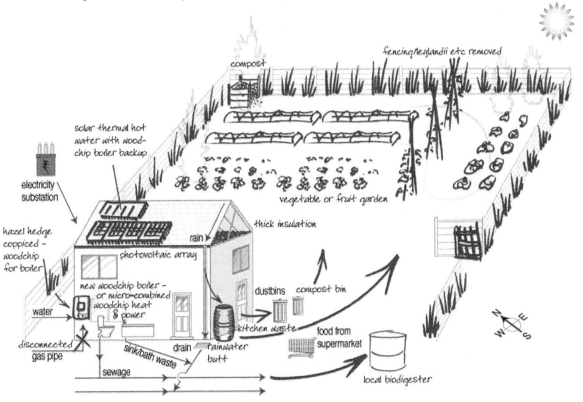

As examples, there is rainwater harvesting, porous surfaces to reduce surface water run off, passive solar heating, heat recovery, a woodchip boiler, perhaps fruit trees for shade, food and enjoyment- even more 'controversial' ideas such as composting toilets. Why not really have fun and compliment a grass roof with some goats, and add wall niches for birds to nest in? The house behaves much more like a 'tree in a forest'. The idea of waste is challenged.

Figure 5.4: Modified cut away of suburban house

On one level it's adult and a caricature but it's the possibility, the imagination which has been triggered by taking the tree as the model and asking how does that work so well? On another level, as the Bill Dunster Zero-energy home illustrates, this is already the near future. This house 'meets the top level (Code 6) of the UK Government's Code for Sustainable Buildings, *which all new housing will have to meet from 2016* (emphasis added). Although connected to the National Grid, the ruralZED house is designed to go through the whole year without drawing on the grid for any power whatsoever.

LIFE'S PRINCIPLES
© BIOMIMICRY GUILD

Operating Conditions
- Earth is in a state of dynamic non-equilibrium
- Earth is water based
- Earth is subject to limits and boundaries

Cellular and nested

Shape rather than material

Resourceful and opportunistic

Simple, common building blocks

Free energy

Antenna, signal, response — Feedback loops

Learns and imitates

Locally attuned and responsive (runs on information)

Integrates cyclic processes

Cross-pollination and mutation

Diverse

Resilient

Decentralized and distributed

Redundant

Fitting form to function

Using multi-functional design

Recycling all materials

Optimizing rather than maximizing

Fostering cooperative relationships

Leveraging interdependence

Self-organizing

Using benign manufacturing

Using life-friendly materials

Using self-assembly

Using water-based chemistry

LIFE CREATES CONDITIONS CONDUCIVE TO LIFE

LIFE ADAPTS AND EVOLVES

Life's Principles Butterfly. Credit: Biomimicry Guild

Biomimicry (from *bios*, meaning life, and *mimesis*, meaning to imitate) is a new science that studies nature's best ideas and then imitates these designs and processes to solve human problems. Studying a leaf to invent a better solar cell is an example of this 'innovation inspired by nature.'

"The conscious emulation of life's genius is a survival strategy for the human race, a path to a sustainable future. The more our world looks and functions like the natural world, the more likely we are to endure on this home that is ours, but not ours alone."
Biomimicry Institute

Ideas for teaching about biomimicry at
http://tinyurl.com/44dmw5

Japan's bullet train and biomimetic design

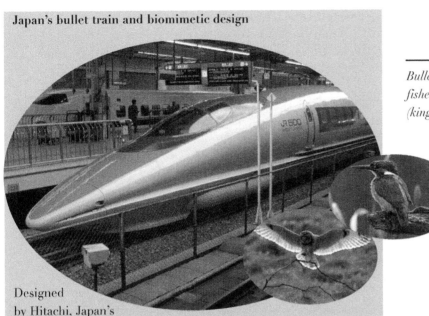

Designed by Hitachi, Japan's 500 series Shinkansen bullet train is one of the fastest in the world (top speed 200 mph). So that it can run quietly at high speeds, the designers mimiced one of the quietest birds, owls. By designing small serrations similar to those on owl feathers, Hitachi have been able to reduce the noise generated by the train's pantograph – the part that connects to overhead electrical wires. The most important biomimetic design feature is the train's nose cone, which is modelled on a kingfisher's beak. This allows the bird to dive from air into water with minimum resistance. On a train, the aerodynamic design reduces the sonic boom that occurs when the train passes from a tunnel back into the open air, reducing noise pollution.

Source: Biomimicry Institute/BusinessWeek, 2008 www.biomimicryinstitute.org

For older students, designing a new house or settlement could be a further stage, with students researching against specific 'cradle to cradle' criteria and critiquing them – for example, the eco-village development of Huangbaiyu, China has been very problematical.

Example Design Criteria

'Cradle to Cradle Design, as envisaged by MBDC[4] is based on the living model for sustainability – nature. The flow and cycling of matter in nature does not lead to waste and pollution, but to a dynamic balance of growth and change within ecological systems. The elements of cradle to cradle design are based on the principles that drive these systems in nature:

Waste equals food
- Design materials and products that are food for other systems. This means designing materials and products to be used over and over in either technical or biological systems.
- Design materials and products that are safe. Design materials and products whose life cycle leaves a beneficial legacy for human or ecological health.
- Create and participate in systems to collect and recover the value of these materials and products.

Use current solar income
- The quality of energy matters. Use renewable energy.

Celebrate diversity
- Water is vital for humans and all other organisms. Manage water use to maximize quality and promote healthy ecosystems while remaining respectful of the local impacts of water use.
- Use social responsibility to guide a company's operations and stakeholder engagement

The house design solutions developed by students can be distinctly modern, like this apartment block for Sweden's eco-municipality, Hammarby Sjöstad (figure 5.5). What is central is the idea of design; sustainability is an intention towards the world not something which is possible by tidying up or as an afterthought. It's that distinction between 'cradle to grave' and 'cradle to cradle' thinking again. Moreover, Amory and Hunter Lovins and others are adamant that trying to adjust just one element of a system can be disastrous for the system as a whole (see 'Housing in Java' box). This is not widely understood but its consequences are all around us.

Figure 5.5: Apartment block Hammarby Sjöstad, Sweden. Credit: Hans Kylberg

"All sustainability is by intention, it is there in the design or it is not there at all. Sustainability is a discussion of beginnings not ends, because the loop is closed. Understanding that and what unfolds from it is the aspiration of education in a green age. In fitting within nature's limits it is not remarkable to imitate nature, it is just what is in front of us. In this way the Teacher is respected and the student cared for – which is simply ancient wisdom from the Tao De Ching brought up to present times."

Sustainability issues overwhelmingly demand a systemic approach, using skills, knowledge and experience from many disciplines. Many schools and colleges carry the evidence of fragmentary thinking dressed up as 'more sustainable' in the very fabric of their buildings. The replacement of leaky windows with pvc double glazed units in pursuit of energy saving and comfort can mean the sealing in of toxic offgassing from furniture, carpets, polishes and plastics, creating an environment up to four times more polluted than a walk in the city street[5]. This is a 'pessimized system', and if the bottom line is staff and students working effectively it is easy to imagine a deterioration in such a 'sick' building.

> **Student Research Activity**
>
> Introduce students to the idea of 'technical' and 'biological' nutrients (see diagram page 27). Ask students to explore school or college, looking for 'technical nutrients' which are being wasted and which could be 'food'. Look for badly designed objects and systems and try to rethink them. What other relationships would have to change to make new systems work well? Would changing just one thing be possible or desirable? Are there always consequences?

Changing the context and scale again, what about food and farming in an era of expensive oil? Bear in mind that natural gas is the main feedstock for nitrogen fertilisers and there is a looming shortage of phosphates too. What do living systems have to say about the possibilities of a farm which is nearly zero input as well as zero waste and zero emissions?

The well respected organic farming and permaculture movement[6] has a lot to say on closing loops and reducing toxicity. The recent reports by the University of Michigan Ann Arbor[7], suggest that a world of 9 billion people can be fed on organic systems – which work particularly well in the developing world – provided we all demand less meat. Currently however, the trend is in the opposite direction as more people achieve higher incomes across the world.

Even getting organic farming systems anywhere near zero fossil fuel input is a huge challenge. Professor George Chan has analyzed one of the most productive farming areas in the world – the Pearl River Delta in China. The Delta sustained an average of 17 people per hectare in the 1980s, a carrying capacity at least ten times the average of industrial farming, and two to three times the world average. Chan brought together what he has learnt to create an Integrated Food and Waste Management System[8] (elements of which can be seen in the 'Cardboard to Caviar' fish farm, see page 91). Mae-Wan Ho from the

Open University and the Institute for Science in Society is working on applying what she calls George Chan's 'Dream Farm 1' model (see figure 5.6) to northern climes under the heading Dream Farm 2[9]. It is an elegant and thorough imitation of living systems in operation, which has the potential to add more animal protein to organic systems and produce marked reductions in climate changing emissions at the same time. It is closed loop thinking par excellence. The key is biodigestion of animal waste.

As explained by Mae-Wan Ho[9], in the Dream farm 1 model the anaerobic digester takes in livestock manure plus wastewater, and generates biogas, which provides all the energy needs for heating,

Figure 5.6: George Chan's Dream Farm 1 model

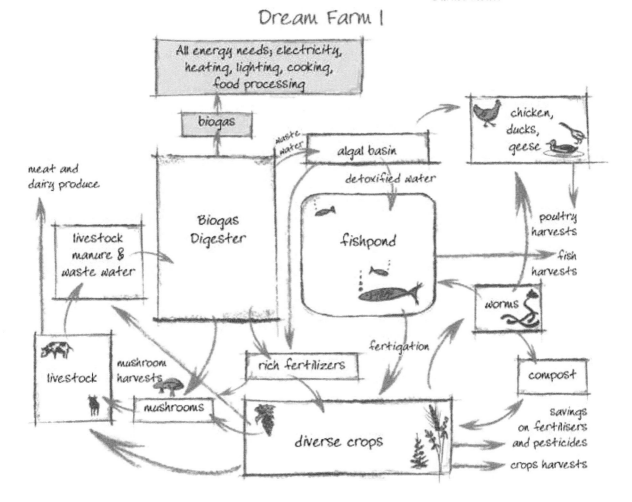

Dream Farm 1

cooking and electricity. The partially cleansed wastewater goes into the algal basin where the algae produce by photosynthesis all the oxygen needed to detoxify the water, making it safe for the fish. The algae are harvested to feed chickens, ducks, geese and other livestock. The fishpond supports a compatible mixture of 5-6 fish species. Water from the fishpond is used to 'fertigate' crops growing in the fields or on the raised dykes. Aquaculture of rice, fruits and vegetables can be done in floats on the surface of the fishpond. Water from the fishpond can also be pumped into greenhouses to support aquaculture of fruits and vegetables. The anaerobic digester yields a residue rich in nutrients that is an excellent fertiliser for crops. It could also be mixed with algae and crop residues for culturing mushrooms after steam sterilisation. The residue from mushroom culture can be fed to livestock or composted. Crop residues are fed back to livestock. Crop and food residues are used to grow earthworms to feed fish and fowl. Compost and worm castings go to condition the soil. Livestock manure goes back into the anaerobic digester, thus closing the grand cycle. The result is a highly productive farm that's more than self-sufficient in food and energy.

Mae-Wan Ho's Dream farm 2 – some principles illustrated
The ideal Dream Farm 2 operates as a UK farm, and also serves as a demonstration, education and research centre, and incubator for new ideas, designs and technologies. Most significant of all, it runs entirely without fossil fuels. Some of the principles of Dream Farm 2 are illustrated on the opposite page. More details at http://tinyurl.com/616gjc

Source: Mae-Wan Ho. Dream farm 2 – a proposal. How to beat climate change and post- fossil fuel economy. Institute of Science in Society (2006).

Dream Farm 1 and 2 reveal some of the potential for food and farming in rural contexts. But students may ask: 'what is the future of urban food in a low carbon world?' If the Dream Farm is not stimulus enough we could encourage learners to evaluate the 'Vertical Farm'[10], or the rooftop garden running on organic hydroponics?[11].

The zero-entropy model of a sustainable system
after Mae-Wan Ho

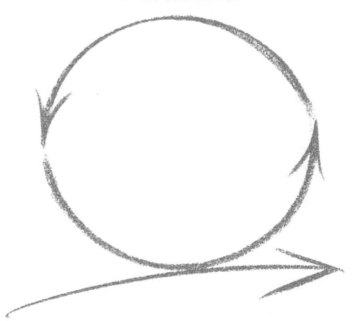

Powered
by the sun

The sustainable system closes the energy and resource use cycle,
maximising storage and internal input and minimising waste, rather like
the life-cycle of an organism that is autonomous and self-sufficient.

Integrated farming system that closes the cycle
thereby minimising input and waste

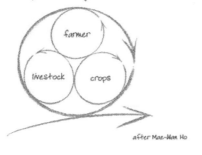

after Mae-Wan Ho

Increasing productivity by incorporating
more lifecycles into the system

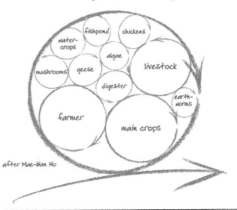

after Mae-Wan Ho

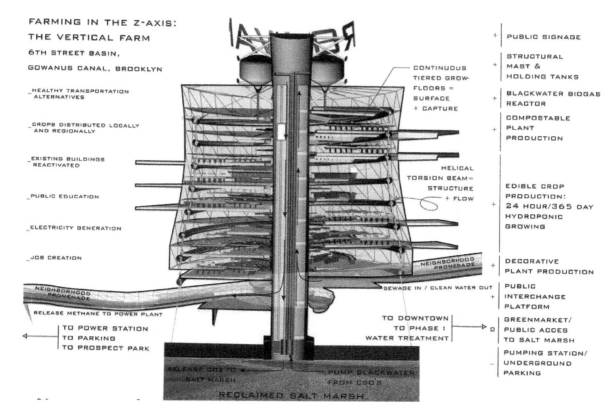

FARMING IN THE Z-AXIS:
THE VERTICAL FARM
6TH STREET BASIN,
GOWANUS CANAL, BROOKLYN

_HEALTHY TRANSPORTATION
ALTERNATIVES

_CROPS DISTRIBUTED LOCALLY
AND REGIONALLY

_EXISTING BUILDINGS
REACTIVATED

_PUBLIC EDUCATION

_ELECTRICITY GENERATION

_JOB CREATION

NEIGHBORHOOD
PROMENADE

RELEASE METHANE TO POWER PLANT

TO POWER STATION
TO PARKING
TO PROSPECT PARK

CONTINUOUS
TIERED GROW-
FLOORS =
SURFACE
+ CAPTURE

HELICAL
TORSION BEAM =
STRUCTURE
+ FLOW

NEIGHBORHOOD
PROMENADE

SEWAGE IN / CLEAN WATER OUT

TO DOWNTOWN
TO PHASE I
WATER TREATMENT

RELEASE CO2 TO
SALT MARSH

PUMP BLACKWATER
FROM CSO'S

RECLAIMED SALT MARSH

+ PUBLIC SIGNAGE

+ STRUCTURAL
MAST &
HOLDING TANKS

+ BLACKWATER BIOGAS
REACTOR

+ COMPOSTABLE
PLANT
PRODUCTION

+ EDIBLE CROP
PRODUCTION:
24 HOUR/365 DAY
HYDROPONIC
GROWING

+ DECORATIVE
PLANT PRODUCTION

+ PUBLIC
INTERCHANGE
PLATFORM

0 GREENMARKET/
PUBLIC ACCES
TO SALT MARSH

− PUMPING STATION/
UNDERGROUND
PARKING

Figure 5.7: Vertical farm. Credit: Dickson Despommier Vertical Farm Group

Once more, these 'farms' are based on an understanding of the waste=food idea and closed loops so far as possible. Here of course there is also a need to factor in advanced engineering, building design and construction, as well as heating and ventilation systems.

The educational message is clear enough – in an era of transition we will be remaking the economy, probably very rapidly, and to do this the notion of exploring, critiquing and debating possibilities is central.

By analogy, this transition could resemble one in a habitat which has recently been damaged by strong winds. Conditions have changed. At such times there is an opportunity for new and rapid growth – to be lyrical: seeds scattered years ago emerge like poppies and daisies do, along the disturbed earth of embankments. It is a period in which species which are adapted to new opportunities flourish.

In an era of transition, a central role for education thus emerges – with a premium on innovation and creativity, the rethinking of problems and solutions, rather than on a fitting in to the now eroded mainstream.

In schools and colleges, there will be the growth of more systemic enquiries within subjects and the development of cross disciplinary opportunities to explore sustainable design (of materials, products, systems, buildings, food and the rest) will expand of necessity as a way of reflecting the changing perspective. This cross disciplinary work will all rest on sustainability as a frame of thinking, based we predict on the circular economy, the living systems model for a low carbon world.

"In a world of shrinking resources, those who first recognize the need for sustainability and adopt appropriate strategies will succeed best in future global competition."
Yves Manfrini, Union Bancaire Privée, Switzerland

Living machines

'Living Machines' are ecological waste water treatment systems that mimic processes found in wetland ecosystems. As well as purifying waste water from industry, homes etc Living Machines can also produce beneficial by-products such as edible and ornamental plants, and fish. Aquatic and wetland plants, bacteria, algae, protozoa, plankton, snails, fish and other freshwater species are used in the system to establish effective food webs and provide specific cleansing functions. In temperate climates, the system of tanks, pipes and filters is housed in a greenhouse to raise the temperature, and thus the rate of biological activity. Living Machines have been successfully used for educational purposes to demonstrate to learners how industrial and domestic waste water treatment systems can be designed to mimic nutrient cycling found in natural wetland ecosystems. See Findhorn Foundation website for details on Living Machines

"A 'Living Machine' in Emmen Zoo, Netherlands filters and cleans 260,000 gallons of wastewater per day using nothing but plants. The water that comes out is drinkable."

Living Machine. Credit: L.Schnadt/Findhorn Foundation http://tinyurl.com/5htcb6

And if this creativity and industry doesn't happen here then it will surely emerge in India or China where the 'circular economy' is a major plank of their ambitions (if not their practice at present) and where, recalling Chapter 1, William McDonough is working alongside the Chinese government and designing six cities on this basis.

Thomas Friedman in his hugely influencial book *The World is Flat*, discusses the impact of new technologies and the global village on employment and innovation in the richer nations. As a snapshot, while almost half a million engineering graduates emerge each year from India and China, the number of UK students opting for engineering is static at around twenty four thousand. Let's turn all this on its head. Here is Gus Speth[12] founder of the Natural Resources Defense Council and the World Resources Institute:

"If you want to hear something really radical, the really radical proposition is that we can make it just continuing to do what we do today. That's a really radical proposition, that business as usual will suffice, because if we just keep doing what we're doing today, releasing the same amounts of greenhouse gases, the same impoverishment of ecosystems, the same toxification, you know, well in the latter part of this century the planet won't be fit to live on."

Do we want to lead transition to a low carbon future or just follow on? That seems to be the choice. For the more hard headed educational leaders it can be just such a practical question, about jobs, careers and prospects. Reason enough for change... But surely we should be approaching transition to a low carbon economy with a grander intention. Here is York University teacher and teacher trainer James Pitt:

"As a teacher I want to engage my students in the discussing of real issues of social, economic and ecological justice and the relationships between these. I want the curriculum, school ethos and relationships with the wider community 'outside' the school all to be informed by these discussions. Indeed the UK government's policies on Every Child Matters, Sustainable Schools and Extended Schools all invite me to do just this.

Yet schools as systems were not designed to facilitate such debate. Individual subject curricula militate against it, as do the endless grinds of

Chapter 5

Standard Assessment Tests, reporting and league tables. The day-to-day burdens of administration can wear any teacher down. It is not clear that schools can provide the territory for radical reappraisal.

Yet within every school there are small components or subsystems that are potential spaces for real education for sustainability. Some subjects, being relatively free of prescribed content, can adopt sustainability as a 'frame of mind'[13] that shapes their whole schemes of work and departmental ethos (an obvious example is Design & Technology). The new Key Stage 3 framework encourages radically new ways of doing things, including cross-curricular activity:

- *Individual teachers can use individual lessons to raise issues of sustainability and justice.*

- *There is actually no part of school life than cannot be connected some way or other with education for sustainable development.*

- *I believe that if we pick up this baton we will reconnect with our original vision and motivation in training to teach."*

Chapter 6 discusses how change extends to notions of schooling and education and to the institutions of schools and colleges themselves.

SIGNPOSTS
**Schools, Colleges and Community Choices*
In this CPD activity participants draw on a base map of the town their ideas for a much more sustainable, low carbon economy (and the place of their school or college). Ideas are tested against a quick checklist as a prompt for further discussion which opens up the myriad choices and uncertainties and the need to bring together knowledge from many different disclipines.

Download the full *Community Choices* activity at
www.senseandsustainability.com.

**Sustainable Food Resources
For extensive sustainable food and farming school case studies and
resources see the Food for Life Programme in schools in England see
http://tinyurl.com/4vdhtz
The Yorkshire&Humber Sustainable Food Education Programme
has developed free education resources exploring how our food
choices have an impact on people and the planet. Download from
http://tinyurl.com/437g3f

***Online streamed or downloadable film shorts, animations and still images
for ESD work*[14]
A wealth of short films on sustainable development issues are downloadable at http://www.green.tv Short films featuring leading
sustainability thinkers and practitioners are to be found on
http://www.bigpicture.tv

See note 14 for more details on web-based images.

Chapter 6

The future – towards the Sustainable school or college.

Figure 6.1: A long road. Early passive solar architecture. St George's School Wallasey, UK. 1961

A low carbon future and our increasingly networked society will not leave schools and colleges unchanged. Just as business and employment, shopping and suburbia will be changed so will arrangements for learning. Educators have a critical role to play in the transition to a low carbon economy. According to David Orr, we need to: "equip our students with the practical skills, analytic abilities, philosophical depth and moral wherewithal to remake the human presence in the world. In short order, as history measures these things, they must replace the extractive economy with one that functions on current sunlight, eliminates the concept of waste, uses energy and materials with great efficiency, and distributes wealth fairly within and between generations. We will have to recast the systems by which we provision ourselves with food, energy, water, materials and livelihood, and by which we handle our wastes...."

Without doubt David Orr sets out a major challenge – the journey to a truly sustainable school could be long and difficult. Sustainability, roughly speaking, would be at least a school with zero carbon impacts and hopefully 'restorative' to both environment and social capital (an 'eco-restorative' school perhaps...). It would be consciously enabling the transition to a low carbon economy through developing critical thinking skills and practical application in school and community.

That's probably enough of an ambition for now! In the table in figure 6.2 we describe a number of stages as a discussion prompt, with *our* sense of the possible phasing of change. Change isn't very tidy and a point we'd like to add is that ESD seen primarily as an adjunct and reinforcement to a school's *environmental management policy* is not what most people had in mind when they considered an education for sustainability. So the table in figure 6.2 adopts the '3Cs' of Curriculum, Campus and Community found in the UK Government's Sustainable Schools' Programme (see figure 6.3).

Stage 1

Individually or as an eco-team activities in school are developed with whatever few resources and money are available. This stage tends to be uncritical and if the curriculum element means anything it is reinforcing a 'do with less' , recycle, you've-heard-it-before list of handy hints and small projects. This is fine when exploring Stage 1. It's a moral agenda really, and focussed on individual behaviour change. Community involvement or outreach is there but more or less on a project basis. Work at stage 1 can generate real enthusiasm but it's probably big on frustration too.

Stage 2

Is money finding its way from the school and college managers into the day to day or term to term purchasing: lightbulbs, energy supply choices, carbon offsetting, paper and so forth? If schools are not reaching into their bank accounts it's a fair estimate that sustainability is not being assimilated. In the community, more permanent features emerge such as shared gardening, reuse and recycling schemes, openness to the community. In the curriculum, the social and economic aspects of the issues are investigated, as well as choices about commitment to (individual) action. This might bring some tensions as the simple 'to do' lists of Stage 1 become critiqued. Is recycling a good idea? Should prices reflect full costs? What's in it for me? Will this add up anyway?

Stage 3

At this stage, school and college take a strategic view using capital projects to obtain major cuts in say carbon emissions (at least 60%). The building now has the potential to support pedagogy – it exemplifies and sets the context for the school's operation which then filters through (let's say) into a mutual exchange between school and community – local food suppliers, selling/buying surplus electricity or sharing water treatment facilities or a car club and so forth. The school is helping counter the loss of social capital. In the curriculum, the job might be a great deal tougher. Perhaps the role and usefulness of essentially 'closed loop' models is demonstrated through the campus and enters mainstream curricula as a debate in design and technology, business, science, humanities and economics. Meanwhile, the overall sense in the school is of discussing the transition to a low carbon future with the community and the choices that need to be made. Learning for change. Many students see this as aspirational as new skills and job opportunities unfold and the school/college refurbishment shows what can be achieved.

Figure 6.2: Sustainable schools and colleges – not yet! Stories around four stages

	Curriculum	Campus	Community
Stage 1 **Exploratory** Small scale enthusiast led activities 'I care, at least!'	'Bolt-on' class activities. Protect Nature. Basic science of issues and mostly 'personal' choices and actions about 'solutions'	'Do your individual bit', recycling, litter picking. Personal eco-footprint	Will you contribute? Can we help? One off community projects
Stage 2 **Assimilating** 'We probably should folks.'	Assumes 'business as usual but greener and fairer.' Social and economic aspects of big picture questions common and challenging	Management of day-to-day spending choices eg purchasing, energy. School eco footprint (audit). 3Rs re school goods procurement	School as a community resource, higher profile for environmental and sustainability aspects school gardens with community involvement etc
Stage 3 **Strategic** 'We know why we will...'	A focus on the roles of business and government as well as the personal. Much interest in 'possible futures' and critical thinking across subjects. Dialogue on meeting new business skills and 'green collar' jobs e.g. design for disassembly, 'systems thinking'	Capital investment. Building as pedagogy. 60% + energy and materials saving. Strategic approach to school travel, water management etc. 'Closed loops' thinking emerges re purchase of goods and services	School as customer and supplier in local community/economy (energy, waste treatment, food?)
Stage 4 **Evolved to 'eco-restorative'** 'We were not immune from the big changes...'	'Systems thinking' a preferred worldview with educators and learners when designing 3Cs programmes. Learning how to learn main activity with content and skills integrated -very personalised? School/college staff share learning facilitation roles with other community stakeholders. Internet learning important.	Re-investment. School concept reshaped by low carbon economy More localisation network school? Eco-Restorative school based on 'closed loops' model? Rethinking of learning spaces	School/community boundary becomes fuzzy. Local community as work, knowledge and skills providers in relation to SD agenda

Stage 4

The sustainability agenda does not leave the *idea* and structure of schooling untouched. How could it? Under many pressures, social and economic as well as environmental, schools evolve and perhaps down-size and relocalise to suit a low carbon economy. The community/ school boundary gets very indistinct with a mix of one to one, local, practical and vocational skills in the community being blended with more part time teaching and ICT based relationships–*a network school*. Systems thinking represents a preferred worldview with educators and learners when designing curriculum, campus and community (3Cs) programmes. The school buildings and campus are possibly 'eco-restorative' – they produce more energy than is used and enhance biodiversity and social capital. Meaning and purpose is enhanced in this evolution. Curriculum is focussed on learning for change (in society) and is highly personalised. The buildings/ manage-ment of learning spaces is responsive, and flexible (see Box).

Pedagogy & Space Matrix - Independent Vs Collaborative

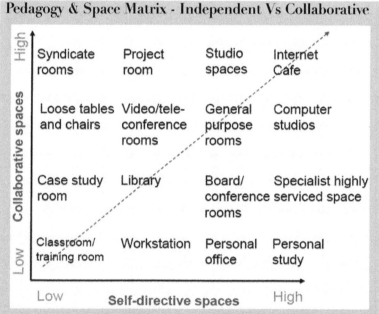

	Collaborative spaces High			
	Syndicate rooms	Project room	Studio spaces	Internet Cafe
	Loose tables and chairs	Video/tele-conference rooms	General purpose rooms	Computer studios
	Case study room	Library	Board/ conference rooms	Specialist highly serviced space
Low	Classroom/ training room	Workstation	Personal office	Personal study
	Low	Self-directive spaces		High

Source: *Are we building sustainable schools? Creating person-alised learning spaces.* Damian Allen, Executive Director of Children's Services, Knowsley Metropolitan Borough Council, 2007. Originally from Dr Kenn Fisher, Rubida Research, University of Melbourne.

Figure 6.3: (below).National Sustainable Schools Framework, England

Doorway	By 2020 DCSF recommends that all schools. . .
Food and drink	*are model suppliers of healthy, local and sustainable food and drink, showing strong commitments to the environment, social responsibility and animal welfare in their food and drink provision, and maximising their use of local suppliers*
Energy and water	*are models of energy efficiency, renewable energy and water conservation, showcasing opportunities such as wind, solar and biomass energy, insulation, rainwater harvesting and grey water recycling to everyone who uses the school*
Travel and traffic	*are models of sustainable travel, where vehicles are used only when absolutely necessary and where there are exemplary facilities for healthier, less polluting or less dangerous modes of transport*
Purchasing and waste	*are models of waste minimisation and sustainable procurement, using goods and services of high environmental and ethical standards from local sources where practicable, and increasing value for money by reducing, reusing, repairing and recycling as much as possible*
Buildings and grounds	*make visible use of sustainable design in their buildings, and develop their grounds in ways that help pupils learn about the natural world and sustainable living*
Inclusion and participation	*are models of social inclusion, enabling all pupils to participate fully in school life while instilling a long-lasting respect for human rights, freedoms, cultures and creative expression*
Local well-being	*are models of corporate citizenship within their local areas, enriching their educational mission with activities that improve the environment and quality of life of local people*
Global dimension	*are models of global citizenship, enriching their educational mission with activities that improve the lives of people living in other parts of the world.*

Credit: Department of Children, Schools and Families, 2008

Figure 6.4 below gives an illustration of a school working at stage 3 and 4 – in transition to a full learning community. Note that the learner has access to many kinds of learning and support within and outside the campus. School/college staff share the learning facilitation roles with other stakeholders in the local community – and beyond. Notice the critical role of personalised and internet based learning.

Figure 6.4: Schools and colleges in transition to a full learning community[1]

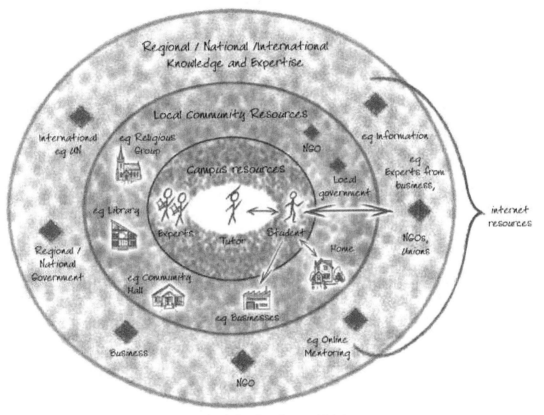

Figure 6.4: Schools and colleges in transition to a full learning community[1]

What a learning community must not be is local and parochial: it must offer connections to the whole global village, as much as face to face mentoring and training. This is now possible. Today's ubiquitous information technologies – and the internet is barely 15 years old in its common web based sense – means that major obstacles to Ivan Illich's 1972 aspiration for a 'good educational system' are now dissolving.

Figure 6.5: XO from the One Laptop per Child programme

Graham Atwell[2] has discussed the challenge of the newly emerging internet tools – the Web 2.0 technologies. In recent years many young people have established accounts on social networking sites including Bebo, Facebook and YouTube. Services such as Facebook are targeted particularly at students. Such social networking services provide tools for content creation and sharing and for developing networks of friends.

Of course, there is an issue as to how much learning takes place through participation and engagement in social networking sites. However, the failure of education providers to engage with this activity risks schools and colleges becoming much less relevant over time to the cultural discourse of young people and to the way in which young people interact and exchange ideas. The decentralising pressures of a low carbon economy is another force prompting a rethink of the role and structure of educational provision within communities and our wider society. One idea, instead of present schools, is the Community Learning Centre or Hub.

These are support centres open to all ages of learners – at least from the age of 11 upwards. Individual learning plans would be developed through a personal learning environment with the support of facilitators/teachers and using many of the untapped human resources of the community but without assuming a 9-4 attendance. Teams would be localised but could include participants from other community learning centres, specialist tutors and learners from other countries participating through networked communication. Many young people already participate in online communities involving participants from different countries in their leisure time. Projects would include community-based organisations and business enterprises.

In the opposite corner there is the tendency to maintain centralised provision–i.e. control–and just reform or adapt it. There are echoes of the tension between centralised energy supply and decentralised renewables networks or between supermarkets and agribusiness and the organic and local suppliers. A best guess is that provision will be more diverse in future, although like supermarket town centre stores – to keep a retailing analogy – it may be still dominated by relatively few industry players and practices such as the award of certificates and the expectation of full time attendance.

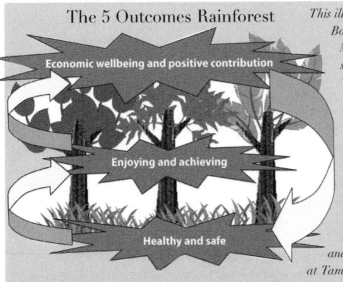

The 5 Outcomes Rainforest

Economic wellbeing and positive contribution

Enjoying and achieving

Healthy and safe

This illustration comes from Tameside Metropolitan Borough Council (MBC) in the UK. Tameside MBC is designing the work programme in their schools to emulate the workings of the rainforest. The UK Government's Every Child Matters Strategy has 5 Outcomes and these are shown here to represent the different rainforest layers – connected in closed loop feedback systems. Limits are a constant reality in the rainforest, yet, paradoxically, scarcity is its own remedy. It triggers constant feedback, learning, and adaptations that shape the organisms and the relationships between organisms so that an extraordinary diversity and richness of life develops. The education team at Tameside MBC is exploring this new business perspective which is now under development in a number of major corporations eg Toyota.

This new approach is demonstrating how organisations can maximise performance and adapt to rapidly-changing market conditions when they become more like nature – like a complex living system.

Source: Ian Smith, Director of Children's Services, Tameside MBC, UK. 2008

It is worth reiterating here how schools and colleges working at Stages 3 and 4 would be aspiring to bring together a coherent model: insights on how nature works; insights on how participative learning works; and insights on how the progressive circular economy is evolving.

As schools begin to synthesise these insights, some valuable advice from Professor Bill Scott in *Sustainability and learning: what role for the curriculum?*:

"Educators have four kinds of responsibility to learners:
1   *to help them understand why a consideration of sustainable development is in their interests;*
2   *to use appropriate pedagogy used for active engagement with issues;*
3   *to help learners gain plural perspectives;*
4   *to encourage learners to continue thinking about such issues beyond their formal education*

In the circumstances, doing less than this seems neglectful; and doing much more suggests an attempt to indoctrinate, which risks rejection and disdain. A fifth responsibility, of course, is to keep an open mind oneself as to what sustainability is. The need is to stimulate without prescribing – and to use conceptual frameworks as support for learning, rather than as restraints on imagination and creativity"

Finally, a playful illustration of an eco-restorative school nested amongst the hills, streams, houses and businesses of its local community. Really, the illustration (see figure 6.6) is just another prompt for discussion about imagining ways to design and develop learning communities within our supporting natural ecosystems. It's an illustration that draws on Figure 6.7 which identifies some indicative questions for senior managers when designing curriculum, campus and community (3Cs) programmes for their eco-restorative school or college.

We make the assumption throughout the book that a Nature as Capital and Nature as Teacher 'systems' framework is *a support for learning* rather than a restraint. It is also useful in the engagement around the first responsibility of educators – 'why a consideration of sustainable development is in (learners) interests' -since it at least models an economy they might aspire to. However, the Nature as Teacher framework is best seen as only a stage in an endless cycle of development, *and is* held firmly enough to be a testing ground for ideas and a counterpoint to the existing conventional wisdom but lightly enough to be superceded or abandoned in due course. It does not of course predict a state called sustainable development, but assists the clarification of thinking which promotes ever more sustainability, or the fit between how Nature and the economy we invent works.

The eco-restorative school or college

The eco-restorative school or college increases the natural and social capital of the location in which it operates as well as access to it. This allows a greater flow of services, materials and energy and increases well-being and participation in the local community.

High efficiency buildings are standard. The buildings might even be energy positive ie the school generates more power than it uses for its traditional functions. This could allow, for example, additional heating of greenhouses and workshops and provide power to allow accelerated waste water treatment and cycling of nutrients (see Living Machine page 117). The eco-restorative school contributes to the optimisation of the local community as a system by acting as one node in a decentralised power grid for example (see figure 6.6), or perhaps as a community workshop space for social enterprises focused on 'repair and reuse' flows of materials.

In landuse terms, the eco-restorative school increases local wildlife diversity through careful planting and habitat management. Recreational access to such areas is encouraged: in urban areas, with limited space, perhaps through the use of flat rooftops as secure gardens. The management of surface water from land around the community is part of local system optimisation.

In curricula, a sustainable school and college has many practical connections to the community. Vocational and training opportunities are tied into how the school and local community operates as eco-restorative – in relation to energy, technology, food, waste-as-food systems, ecology and design, business to name but a few.

Source: Yorkshire&Humber ESD Programme, 2008.

Figure 6.6: Sustainable schools and colleges-Moving through Stages 3 and 4 Credit: Yorkshire&Humber ESD Programme, 2007

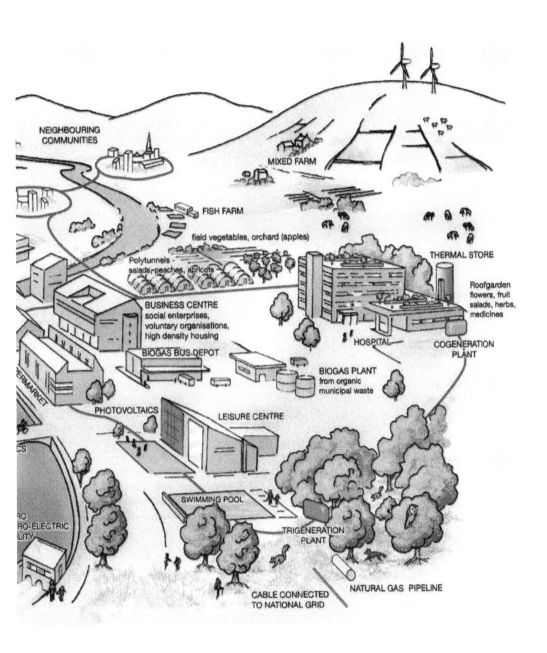

NEIGHBOURING
COMMUNITIES

MIXED FARM

FISH FARM

field vegetables, orchard (apples)

THERMAL STORE

Polytunnels -
salads, peaches, apricots

Roofgarden
flowers, fruit
salads, herbs,
medicines

BUSINESS CENTRE
social enterprises,
voluntary organisations,
high density housing

HOSPITAL

COGENERATION
PLANT

BIOGAS BUS DEPOT

BIOGAS PLANT
from organic
municipal waste

PHOTOVOLTAICS

LEISURE CENTRE

SWIMMING POOL

RO-ELECTRIC
ILITY

TRIGENERATION
PLANT

CABLE CONNECTED
TO NATIONAL GRID

NATURAL GAS PIPELINE

Figure 6.7: Sustainable Schools – some key questions for senior managers when designing curriculum, campus and community programmes for a sustainable school or college

Buildings:
How can we make the school and college more like a tree in the forest? Can we 'close the loop' and keep the energy and other resource flows closer to the school by smart building and refurbishment design? In new building or refurbishment how can we incentivise green design? It could extend to use too... e.g. should staff parking at school be offered at all – or for free? The building as pedagogy. What messages does it send now? What messages should it send?

Energy:
The energy debate still tends to be a lot about supply and too little about demand andffficiency, too often an electricity debate not an energy one. How to best shift the discussion from the electricity to an energy debate?
Often the discussion focus is on centralized electricity grids and plugging in big power stations, too little about devolved energy generation, co generation and multiple sources. How can we shift the debate from the former to the latter? Every home and school a micro-power station?

Food:
What steps do we need to take to develop a more localised food economy less reliant on fossil fuel inputs, conventional fertilisers and pesticides? How can we influence people's purchasing habits so that sustainability is a key factor in their choice of food? How can we reverse the trend of excessive packaging of our food? Is it important that the issues of sustainability as well as price, quality and nutritional value be a key factor in the procurement of food eaten in our schools?

Waste and purchasing:
If ours is a throw-away society, where is 'away'? In a sustainable society, as in Nature, won't waste=food? Prices are messages to buyers and sellers, so why don't they include all environmental and social costs? Most recycling is 'downcycling': the material is degraded and headed for disposal some time soon. When is 'recycling' worthy of the name? If ordinary recycling rates never keep up with increasing consumption of materials what do we need to change? Huge resource savings come from renting not buying (as in carshare schemes, photocopiers, carpets and machinery) So why not light bulbs, washing machines, power drills and fridges as standard? In the future will the customer also be the supplier, as products are taken back as standard at the end of use? Implications for schools/colleges?

Global:
Increasingly, developed countries export waste, especially electronics, paper and plastics to China, ships for breaking to India and so on. It's recycling, creates jobs and uses empty containers which have brought us cheap imported manufactured goods - but is all well? Distance separates us from the people who make many of the things we use.

Social inclusion/participation:
As it affects employment, attainment and crime as well as the quality of life how can social capital be rebuilt-trust be developed, community groups supported and networks expanded? Cheap oil helped distance us from one another–in suburbs, private cars, and from the places and people who make the products we use.

We do not see the farmer/shoemaker or know her and find it hard to care as a result. At the same time endless advertising/marketing creates dissatisfaction – the feeling we are not well off. This also reduces our capacity for thinking of others. How is this circle squared? It is cheap to create and share digitally: music, film, arts-cultural diversity. To what extent is this expanding world wide web enriching the global citizen? Changing the rules of the globalisation game. What about personal carbon allowances, or a Tobin tax, or attending to 'BOP' (bottom of the pyramid) markets? Or leapfrogging the mistakes of the industrialised world? What ideas are interesting and worth discussion in our schools and colleges?

Will expensive oil bring us together? In the digital communication age will schools act more like networks than knowledge centres, drawing on local community expertise and more distant resources in a more flexible and diverse way? As schools become more embedded in their locality when meeting their physical needs (energy, food, materials and waste), to what extent will this increase their interdependence and the importance of the local community?

Travel:
As well as practical measures for reducing the rise in the use of cars and promoting walking, cycling and public transport is there a debate about what is shaping underlying behaviour?

What will be the impact of an end to cheap oil? How might a 'sustainable future' change the function, size and location of 'schools'? When travel and traffic is discussed it can sometimes be too much about personal choices. There's often not enough discussion about systemic or incentivised change:
- how best to use the market and/or setting the 'rules of the game'? (financial incentives/ disincentives to cut carbon emissions-such as road pricing, fuel prices)
- what about the roles and responsibilities of business and government (as well as individuals)?

Credit: Yorkshire & Humber ESD Programme, 2009.

Figure 6.8: Writers Walk , Sydney Harbour.

It is near the end of this particular journey. Chapter 7 is an overview and summary. The thought which comes most to our minds, apart from the awareness that there is so much more to discuss and describe, is the sense that faced with a shift to a low carbon economy, as part of a bigger shift to a credibly sustainable world, we will do more and move faster when we combine clear ideas with practical activity. The result can be William Stahel's cathedral building, not just piles of cut stones. It won't be an easy or tidy process but as novelist James Michener observed drily:

"Mankind was destined to live on the edge of perpetual disaster.
We are mankind because we survive.
We do it in a half assed way, but we do it."

Chapter 7

Worldviews Matter – Sense and Sustainability

It may be that universal history is the history of a handful of metaphors

Jorge Luis Borges

As a rule we disbelieve all the facts and theories for which we have no use.

William James

Nuclear fusion?

Our Sun. Credit: NASA

The economy is not yet closed loop, far from it. But linear systems can only work with buried sunshine and unrestrained waste while the energy lasts and the environment allows. Barring nuclear fusion, or some as yet unseen alternative, the economy has to fall in line.

When asked at a White House presentation about clean nuclear power as an option, William McDonough replied:

"I'm a big fan of clean nuclear power, and of fusion, I think we should spend trillions of dollars capturing fusion energy immediately. And thank God we have our nuclear reactor exactly where we want it, 93 million miles away – just 8 minutes – and it's tireless."

This chapter is an expansion on the main themes and schemas in the poster *Sense and Sustainability*, but it should read well on its own if the poster is not to hand.

This book has been about the importance of frameworks for thinking. In the transition to a low carbon economy some frameworks may work better than others. These frameworks appear to be largely unconscious and metaphorical. When asked to put it at its simplest in a workshop one of us drew an arrowed straight line followed by a loop. It's a shift from seeing the world as linear – the take-make-and-dispose to one which has closed the loop, where waste=food.

It is also a shift from particulars, seeing the grains of sand neatly separated, as compared to seeing the flow of the sand and identifying eddies and vortices as the parts. The part is embedded, and context matters. Context provides meaning.

The eye uses both detailed and peripheral vision to bring us information about what we see. If detailed vision is lost through damage to the eye then we can still make some sense of what we see. If peripheral vision is lost we literally can't make sense of what we see. Context matters.

Figure 7.1: Grains of sand

So does feedback. Feedback is essential for learning, it makes systems less stupid, which is a good thing. In the linear economy only things with a price are part of the feedback loop. The environment and society usually do not have a price, though they have a value. The results we know more about now.

Figure 7.2: Hurricane vortex and spiraling clouds over Yucatan Peninsula, Mexico. Credit: NASA

Figure 7.3: Car exhaust cartoon

One way to encourage consumer demand for clean cars :-
close the loop and provide feedback !

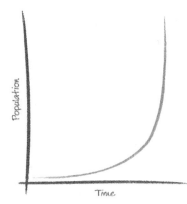

Figure 7.4: Exponential curve

Feedback can also disrupt, as anyone who has left an open microphone too near its loudspeaker will affirm. Change can be amplified very rapidly in closed loops. In a graph it looks like figure 7.4. We have seen many examples of these.

Sustainability is essentially a closed loop notion. It's not rocket science. The best expression of this is Nature: it has a 3.8 billion year track record. Sometimes feedback ran out of control and a great deal of life was extinguished – the five mass extinction events in Earth history, not counting the signs of the sixth, ongoing – but let's not dwell on this.

Hence the notion of Nature as Teacher. Actually, it is probably more complicated than rocket science when you really get into it (see p16) but for now it's a question of perspectives. Alongside Nature as Teacher is Nature as Capital. The economy is a wholly owned subsidiary of the environment, though we tend to act as if this is not the case. The thing about capital is that from it comes a flow of income, something to live upon. But capital is the accumulation of surplus, from the energy of the sun via living things. Social capital too comes from the long learning process which is civilisation. If capital is lost or degraded it provides less income. Capital can be restored or increased too.

What is changing now is that these core ideas about 'how things work' are on the move. The Nature as Teacher, Nature as Capital framework is becoming 'resonant' and resonance is the way one system becomes tuned to another and vibrates in sympathy with it. It can be music-literally. Here are seemingly disparate elements 'resonating':

- How science understands the world – most systems are non linear systems with feedback loops
- Teaching and learning – participative learning depends on feedback
- How Nature works – living systems are looped and interdependent
- How business aspires to work – moving rapidly to the cradle to cradle model: because waste is a sign of bad management which adds to costs and damages profits, especially in a world of resource limits.

Chapter 7

We decided to use the simple analogy of the fruit machine and a winning row of cherries in the poster, to show the Nature as Teacher, Nature as Capital framework 'lining up'. It harks back to the cherry tree (see p49 and the box below).

Figure 7.5: Row of cherries. Credit: Diego Infante

Back to the Cherry Tree
"Eco-effectiveness seeks to design industrial systems that emulate the healthy abundance of nature. The central design principle of eco-effectiveness is waste equals food.

Instead of directing intelligence towards regulation, compliance and liability reduction, why not design industrial processes and products so safe they do not need regulation, and direct creativity towards maximizing economic, social, and ecological benefits? Eco-effectiveness has profound implications for industries everywhere. Rather than lamenting a world of hazardous waste, scarce resources, and limited opportunities, it celebrates an abundance of continuously valuable industrial and natural materials, of rich and diverse living systems, of economic and environmental wealth.

The eco-effective future of industry is a 'world of abundance' that celebrates the use and consumption (by people, nature, and intelligent industrial systems) of products and materials that are, in effect, nutritious – as safe, effective, and delightful as a cherry tree."
William McDonough

"*Nike was attacked in 1994 for poisoning people in Vietnam. The traditional human rights people said, 'Oh, the workers need to wear masks.' The traditional environmental people said, 'Nike needs to make filters and treatments.' I said, 'No. They need to use the right materials.'*"

Michael Braungart

How about the school or college?

If the Nature as Teacher, Nature as Capital framework appears useful, it will be used. Educationally, we feel it is useful because it helps create potentially more coherent discussion about the possibilities of the future. It helps give a sense of sustainability as a hopeful enterprise. It can be a way of testing ideas as well as a generator of ideas. It seems useful because it frames existing problems differently.

Take for example that age old issue of litter. Existing perspectives tend to be based around coaxing the individual to behave differently, 'more responsibly,' or about schemes for the collection and sorting of litter for some notion of recycling. This is basically a linear model with waste reduction options.

How might ESD work around litter look with a waste=food perspective? A series of questions could be developed with learners. Here they are in adult terms for brevity:

Why aren't wrappers compostable?

How does disposing of potentially valuable, expensive, often oil-based resources in landfill or an incinerator make business sense? Why?

What is the real price of the packaging and why isn't this included in the cost? If it was, what might happen to the prices and behaviour of the firms?

Does recycling always make sense – in energy and resource terms, for wrappers and the many sorts of packets and bottles we have?

Perhaps all non-compostable waste has to go back to the producer – as a potential 'technical nutrient' – is it possible, and how would that change things? Or could they be made 'biological nutrients' instead?

As a discussion point let's say that the school or college shop or cafeteria has to accept back all and any packaging it sells – the product is sold to customers at a profit after all. If the shop or café doesn't get all the packaging back it has to collect it up. Close the loop on the business model. It's part of their costs isn't it? *How does the shop or café react?*

Chapter 7

Or if packaging was awarded a local price – like the old deposit on a bottle scheme – and all packaging could be changed for cash or other goods *what would happen?*

Is this practical? Why not just stick to Plan A – regulation and moral pressure. After all, the staff and students dropped the litter. But just 'tidying up' misses so much.

This developed discussion about packaging and litter matters because the context is assumed to be about education for sustainability, not cleaning up the playground. There is no better illustration of the difference between ESD and environmental management. Just cleaning up, Plan A, accepts the ends as given, it provides limited learning. One questionable lesson is that litter is a consumer responsibility, and that some people are falling short–a moral argument essentially–or that obligations to pick it up might be avoided–with some luck! Meanwhile the endless frippery of packaging and marketing, the role of retailer and manufacturer, or government is not addressed. It says it's down to us and having failed or fallen short we then deserve what is coming.

*What about tidying up the litter **and** sending it off in protest to the manufacturers?*

A good start... and what advice would our students attach in a letter to the manufacturer (with a cc to government)?

Students exploring a cradle to cradle framework might draw attention to the arrival of the end of cheap oil and the 'take-make-dump' economy... and the need to mimic nature as we design new industrial products and processes. Students recognise the issue as one of design by human intention.

This cartoon from High Moon (figure 7.6 over page) takes up this shift in perspective. In it the manufacturer poses the problem of what to do with waste to citizens and the public administration. This is the existing situation. But in the future the manufacturers will also be on the panel, sharing responsibility, and *willingly so* as the 'garbage' is in reality a collection of valuable resources which manufacturers will wish to get back. The question will be one of making this process effective, improving the design of the system.

Figure 7.6: High Moon cartoon. On the cartoon caption: yes, good point, but will it ever become garbage? Won't business want these valuable metals back? Perhaps the engine will only be rented to customers in the first place?

Conclusion

Almost any stimulus across campus, community or curriculum can and will generate new questions when a new framework is in play. That is what frameworks do. One of the strengths of schools, colleges and education professionals is their ability to adapt work to their own purposes. What *Sense and Sustainability* has sought to do is simplify and codify that task so that professional development, with its own emphasis on participative enquiry based work, has a choice of *a different but coherent context within which to operate*. This brings us full circle, appropriately enough, and what is revealed from that process will not be determined but it will, with luck, now have a richer meaning.

Afterword. And what do we do now?

During the book review process we were asked to draw some of the threads together, to help with next steps. In many ways *Sense and Sustainability* has been an overview and much less of a detailed how-to book. That's important, and deliberate, but not the end of the story. Moving from the unsustainable present to a sustainable low carbon future, on a habitable, richly biodiverse and socially inclusive planet requires us to navigate in open water. There is no how-to manual, but there are clues. We hazard six.

Firstly, as Al Gore noted, one of the few things we know is that we must 'Put a Price on Carbon'[1]. The *why* is arguably a core lesson in any ESD and the *how* should be a keen debate.

Secondly, we can be pretty confident that scientific world views are in transition towards an 'ecological worldview', as the leading ecologist Charles Krebs[2] asserts:

"two views of the world dominate our thinking this century....the Ecological World View...contrasts sharply with the polar-opposite Economic World View to which many governments and business leaders subscribe. You are living in a century in which the Economic World View will be superseded by the Ecological World View."

What are the lessons of ecology and Nature? (see p49) We need to know and share the roots (at least) of that understanding as it is the heart of all change. As Einstein once noted: 'the theory determines what we observe.' We now have this more inclusive, scientific framework. Let's use it.

Thirdly, we can be confident that sustainability is a systems issue and that, again, in the words of Al Gore:

"As important as it is to change the lightbulbs it's more important to change the laws... in order to solve the climate crisis we have to solve the democracy crisis."

Bottom line: it is a citizenship question first, and not a consumer one. The balance of work in schools and colleges needs reviewing so that it is also *more* about 'systems and citizenship' and *less* about 'me and consumerism.'

Not another checklist. Just some things to look out for on your travels.

(1) Give Carbon a Price: *Give the World a Chance. Know why and discuss how, (with equity)*

(2) Learn the lessons of Nature: *Cradle to cradle thinking. Know, share and explore though an ecological world view. How does it feel?*

(3) Check for balance: *'Systems and citizenship' more than 'me and consumerism'*

(4) Support a love of ideas and critical thinking (philosophy)

(5) Find suitable business allies: *focus on design and human intention*

(6) Be strategically optimistic: *possibilities as well as challenges. A heroic response?*

Fourthly, and relatedly, is the evidence that we live in a culture of distraction, of fleeting attention and disconnection – of 'me-ism'. Programmes such as *Philosophy for Children*[3] encourage careful thinking, and the enjoyment of ideas. Ideas themselves are important, mere opinion or sentiment, left unchallenged, leads nowhere – it's part of the 'me-ism'. Sustainability, as William McDonough reminds us, is about human intention. An ecological worldview offers re-connection, the possible recovery of meaning, and rebuilding social capital. For some, the chance of a more authentic life.

Fifthly, all of this requires connecting with business as well as ecology. As Jonathon Porritt and others note, capitalism is the only game in town at the moment and sustainability won't be achieved without business. As we have seen, innovative business is already ahead when it comes to thinking through resource issues. This is not to be naïve. We have been equally aware of the greenwashing and double standards but finding business partners who know their closed loops – like InterfaceFLOR – is on the mark for credibility with students and colleagues alike. It is about anticipating a green collar economy. Design and technology departments will probably lead the way with enthusiasm. Some already are. This is good news for business itself.

Sixthly, there is the question of optimism, strategic optimism: it can be done. Schellnhuber, one of Europe's leading climate scientists[4], sees a successful 1% a year fall in emissions leading to stability. NASA's Jim Hansen is similarly optimistic that we can engineer changes to bring CO_2 levels back to safe limits[5] given political will.

Figure 7.7: Example Optimism-TREC. The key technology for tapping into solar energy is 'concentrating solar power'(CSP) which normally means using mirrors to concentrate sunlight to create heat. The heat may be used to raise steam to drive turbines and generators in the conventional way or it may drive Stirling engines with generators. Using High Voltage Direct Current means low losses. Result: a renewables supergrid. All the technology is available now[6]. Credit: The Club of Rome.

Amory Lovins published a peer reviewed and costed strategy for 'winning the oil end-game' back in 2005[7]. It's free to download or just watch his TED presentation[1 ibid] and download the slides: the point being that there is no reason why we should not actively balance the understanding of the challenges ahead with an understanding of the real possibilities for a bright green future.

Ken Webster and Craig Johnson

Contribute

Exploring new avenues in ESD and interested in sharing these with others? The Sense and Sustainability website at www.senseandsustainability.com is a source of support and lesson ideas as well as a place for practitioners and managers to disseminate the results of their own work. The number printed at the base of this page is sufficient to log in to the members part of the site.

Acknowledgements

It is not possible to mention all the individuals who have helped with this book. We have benefited from the work of many who have preceded us, as well as those we consider our colleagues in this work

Thanks to teacher colleagues for creative discussion and exchange of ideas in ESD workshops over the years. We would particularly like to thank the following people for their valuable comments and advice on the book drafts:

Carolyn Barraclough (Head of Geography, Abbey Grange High School, Leeds)

John Edwards (Headteacher) and Patricia Harwood (Sustainable Development manager, Lower Fields Primary School, Bradford);

John Hartshorne (Head of Biology, Queen Elizabeth School, Hexham);

Catherine Johnson (Arts Officer, Craven District Council)

Becky Neason (Business Studies Teacher, Prospect School, Reading)

Dick Palfrey (School Improvement Officer, Kirklees Learning Service)

James Pitt (MA in ESD course leader, Department of Educational Studies, University of York);

Katie Sutton (Schools Carbon Management Officer, Calderdale Metropolitan Borough Council);

Caroline Walker (Monkton Wyld Education Centre/former Head, Small School, Devon)

Rob Walker (Vice Principal, Huddersfield New College).

We also acknowledge the organisations that have supported and helped to shape our work: University of Manchester; University of Bradford; WWF UK; Field Studies Council; Particular thanks to Yorkshire Forward for their support of the Yorkshire&Humber ESD Programme. Also Yorkshire&Humber ESD Forum Management Group.

Thanks to Hiroshi Takatsuki (Pen-name: High Moon) Professor, Ishikawa Prefectural University; his images courtesy of Japan for Sustainability at http://www.japanfs.org/en/cartoon/index.html

Special thanks to our book designer/layout Debbie Oakes and to David Shrigley, for the use of *One Day a Big Wind Will Come* as the cover image (www.davidshrigley.com) and to Plenty Magazine for the use of the image *Unlikely Environmentalists* on the back cover.

Selected Bibliography

Capra, F. (1999) *Ecoliteracy: The Challenge for Education in the Next Century*, Centre for Ecoliteracy, Schumacher Series, Liverpool, CA.

Datschefski, E. (2001) *The Total Beauty of Sustainable Products*, Rotovision Books.

Goldring, A. editor. (2000) *Permaculture Teachers' Guide*, *Permaculture Association/WWF UK*

Greig, S., Pike G. and Selby, D. (1989) *Greenprints for Changing School*, World Wide Fund for Nature /Kogan Page, Godalming.

Hawken, P., Lovins, A.B. and Lovins, L.H. (1999) *Natural Capitalism: Creating the Next Industrial Revolution*, Little, Brown, New York

McDonough, W. and Braungart, M. (2002) *Cradle to Cradle: Remaking the Way We Make Things*, Farrar, Straus and Giroux, New York

Orr, D.W. (1994) *Earth in Mind: On Education, Environment, and the Human Prospect*, Island Press, Washington DC.

Porritt, J. (2005) *Capitalism as if the World Matters*. London: Earthscan

Schwartz, B. (2004) *The Paradox of Choice: Why More is Less*, HarperPerrenial, New York

Steffan, A. editor. (2006) *World Changing: A User's Guide for the 21st Century* HNA

Sterling, S. (2004) *Linkingthinking New Perspectives on Thinking and Learning for Sustainability*, WWF Scotland, Aberfeldy.

Vare, P. and Scott, W. (2007) *Learning for a Change: exploring the relationship between education and sustainable development*, Journal of Education for Sustainable Development, volume 1, no.2,191-198.

Webster, K. (2004) *Rethink, Refuse Reduce... Education for Sustainability in a Changing World*, FSC, Shrewsbury

Webster, K. (2007) *Changing the story: 'Cradle-to-cradle' thinking as a compelling framework for ESD in a globalised world* Int. J. Innovation and Sustainable Development, Vol. 2, Nos. 3/4, p282-299

Acknowledgements

Wessels, T. (2006) *The Myth of Progress – Towards a Sustainable Future*, University of Vermont Press, Burlington.

WorldWatch Institute (2008) *State of the World 2008*, WW Norton, London

Selected websites

http://www.forumforthefuture.org.uk/
http://www.worldchanging.com
http://www.treehugger.com
http://earthtrends.wri.org/
http://www.worldwatch.org/
http://john.huckle.org.uk/
http://www.biothinking.com/

Chapter notes and references

Introduction

(1) Our preference is for the term education for sustainability but we use this interchangeably with education for sustainable development (or 'ESD') throughout

(2) David Orr *The Case for the Earth*, Resurgence, Issue 219. July/August 2003
http://www.resurgence.org/resurgence/issues/orr219.htm

(3) G.Lakoff and M.Johnson, *Philosphy in the Flesh*, Basic Books Inc. (1999)

Chapter 1

(1) Including using antibiotic-producing bacteria to control parasites in their fungus gardens

(2) Yes, there is the second law of thermodynamics–energy has to come from somewhere and the entropy or disorder of the universe increases overall.

(3) As proposed by Haug et al *Influence of the intertropical convergence zone on the East Asian monsoon* Nature vol 445, p 74

(4) G.Lakoff and M.Johnson, *Philosphy in the Flesh*, Basic Books Inc. p3 (1999)

(5) What about the academic wars between postmodern and analytic philosophy?
LAKOFF: The results suggest that both sides were insightful in some respects and mistaken in others. The postmodernists were right that some concepts can change over time and vary across cultures. But they were wrong in suggesting that all concepts are like that. Thousands are not. They arise around the world in culture after culture from our common embodiment. Postmodernists were right in observing that there are many places where the folk theory of essences fails (the idea that every entity has an essence or nature, a collection of attributes that makes it the kind of thing that it is). But they were wrong in suggesting that such a failure undercuts our conceptual systems and makes them arbitrary. .. Although formal logic does not work for all, or even most, of reason, there are places where something akin to formal logic (much revised) does characterize certain limited aspects of reason. But the analytic tradition was wrong in certain of its central theses: the correspondence theory of truth, the theory of literal meaning, and the disembodied nature of reason.

Source: The Edge www.edge.org/3rd_culture/lakoff/lakoff_p4.html

Chapter 2

(1) Based on the essay *Winning the Great Wager* by Alex Steffen
http://www.worldchanging.com/archives/002197.html

(2) Source *The Story of Stuff* http://www.storyofstuff.com

(3) Clive Hamilton and Richard Denniss *Affluenza: When too much is never enough* Allen & Unwin (2006)

"here's this constant desire to renew what we have to replace one set of stuff with a new set of stuff."

(4) Recycled PET bottles are often spun into fibres rather than made into new plastic bottles. This is because plastic loses its quality when recycled and so it is preferable to make a product with a long life such as a fleece jacket rather than a product that will need recycling many times such as a bottle.

(5) Jeff Vail *Efficiency Policy, Jevon's Paradox, and the "Shadow" Rebound Effect* http://www.theoildrum.com/node/2499

(6) From Amory Lovins et al *Natural Capitalism* but also found with additional useful notes at http://www.interfacesustainability.com/nat-cap.html

(7) Widely accessible e.g. http://www.rebelsell.com/ and http://www.harpercollins.ca/rs/qa.asp. Note also

"as a program for solving the big environmental problems that we collectively face, the 'think globally/act locally' slogan is completely unhelpful. Most of the big problems-acid rain, groundwater pollution, global warming-will not be affected by local consumer-based action. They require large-scale international institutional cooperation, which can only be achieved through long, difficult political negotiations."

(8) *A Well Being Manifesto for a flourishing society* NEF mini booklet.
http://www.neweconomics.org

(9) Barry Schwarz *The Paradox of Choice*: *Why More is Less*, Harper Perrenial, (2004)

(10) Andrew Szasz *Shopping our way to Safety* University of Minnesota Press (2007)

Within a couple of decades, Szasz reveals, bottled water and water filters, organic food, 'green' household cleaners and personal hygiene products, and 'natural' bedding and clothing have gone from being marginal, niche commodities to becoming mass consumer items. Szasz sees these fatalistic, individual responses to collective environmental threats as an inverted form of quarantine, aiming to shut the healthy individual in and the threatening world out

154

(11) Adam Liptak *1 in 100 U.S. Adults Behind Bars, New Study Says*
http://www.nytimes.com/2008/02/28/us/28cnd-
prison.html?_r=1&oref=slogin

(12) *State of the World 2008*, Worldwatch. This edition of the annual publication has a very strong section on innovation and the sustainable economy. A valuable backgrounder.

(13) R Lloyd *The Commons revisited: the Tragedy Continues* Energy Policy 35 (2007) 5806–5818. The *Unitax* idea for pricing carbon and the relationship between governments and corporations discussed.

"In a nutshell the diagnosis of the ultimate problem is simple, cheap oil and personal greed has enabled corporations to afflict people with affluenza*, and affluenza together with population growth is causing resource depletion and anthropogenic global warming. Solutions relying on mutually acceptable coercion suffer from the difficulty of obtaining any form of mutual acceptance by the people of the world in a situation where world governments are becoming subservient to the free market paradigm and specifically to large corporations." p11 (*Affluenza...is the economics of unfettered consumption, of generation of waste for monetary gain.) p6

(14) http://www.greenmac.com/bioneers/McDonough/

(15) McDonough and Braungart *The Extravagant Gesture (2001)*
http://www.mcdonough.com/writings/extravagant_gesture.htm

Chapter 3

(1) Fritjof Capra *The Web of Life : A New Scientific Understanding of Living Systems.* New York: Anchor Books (1996)

(2) Chris Skrebowski is the Editor of the UK Petroleum Review. "I find that Peak Oil occurs in 2011 plus or minus one year."
http://aspocanada.ca/chris-skrebowskis-open-letter-to-cera.html

(3) 10 kcal of exosomatic energy are required to produce 1 kcal of food delivered to the consumer in the U.S. food system. This includes packaging and all delivery expenses, but excludes household cooking. *Food, Land, Population and the U.S. Economy; Executive Summary,* Pimentel, David and Giampietro, Mario. Carrying Capacity Network, (1994) http://www.dieoff.com/page40.htm see also *Eating Fossil Fuels* an essay by Dale Allen Pfeiffer at
http://www.fromthewilderness.com/free/ww3/100303_eating_oil.html

(4) *"...127 calories of energy (aviation fuel) are needed to transport 1 calorie of lettuce across the Atlantic. If the energy consumed during lettuce*

cultivation, packaging, refrigeration, distribution in the UK and shopping by car was included, the energy needed would be even higher. Similarly, 97 calories of transport energy are needed to import 1 calorie of asparagus by plane from Chile, and 66 units of energy are consumed when flying 1 unit of carrot energy from South Africa."

http://www.321energy.com/editorials/church/church040205.html (with additional references)

(5) *The End of Suburbia Oil Depletion and the Collapse of The American Dream* http://www.endofsuburbia.com/

(6) http://faostat.fao.org/site/339/default.aspx

(7) There is enough waste cooking oil in the UK to meet only one 380th of our demand for road transport fuel. British Association for Biofuels and Oils estimates the available volume at 100,000 tonnes a year.

(8) http://www.celsias.com/2007/10/10/has-the-tipping-point-been-reached-already/

(9) For detail and material about the Schellnhuber Tipping Points (now 16 in number) see http://www.pik-potsdam.de/infodesk/tipping-points Schellnhuber notes

"There is a good chance to avoid such dangerous climate change if the anthropogenic warming is limited to 2°C. This means – above all – that atmospheric greenhouse gas concentrations must be confined, in the long term, to values below 400 ppm C02 equivalence.

This, in turn, requires to reduce industrial greenhouse gas emissions by about 1% per annum throughout this century. Recent socioeconomic analyses, taking technological and institutional innovation into full account, indicate that a reduction would delay global welfare growth till 2100 by just three months.

The confinement of global warming to 2°C and the adaptation to the residual, significant impacts nevertheless asks for a re-invention of modern society that especially defines urbanity and rurality in novel ways."

(10) Energy Watch Group *The Uranium Report* 2006

(11)

http://news.independent.co.uk/uk/this_britain/article2276189.ece

(12) A four part BBC series the *Century of Self* shows up on Google video and other online resources. It appears to be unavailable otherwise.

(13) *13th Tipping Point* by Julia Whitty. This long article also has much to say about the possibilities of motivating individuals http://www.motherjones.com/news/feature/2006/11/13th_tipping_point.html

(14) Richard Heinberg *Peak Oil: Sustainability with Teeth*
http://www.energybulletin.net/3204.html

(15)http://www.paperview.com/store/index.php?main_page=product_info&cPath=27&products_id=819

Chapter 4

(1) Dongtan eco city. Arup Press Office, 2008.

(2) See all the stages of the Interface flor model at http://www.interfacesustainability.com/model.html

(3) Paul Hawken, Amory and Hunter Lovins *Natural Capitalism – the Next Industrial Revolution* Earthscan (1999)

(4) Walter Stahel *From products to services* http://www.greeneconomics.net/Stahel%20Essay1.doc

(5) Tachi Kiuchi and Bill Shireman *What we Learnt in the Rainforest – Business Lessons from Nature* Berrett – Koeler Publishers *(2002)*

(6) H. Thomas Johnson and Anders Broms *Profit beyond Measure* Free Press (2002)

(7) For a summary review of the Toyota management approach see http://www.globalcommunity.org/business/byond_msure.shtml

(8) From the transcript to Thomas Friedman's *Addicted to Oil* (June 2006) http://www.calcars.org/calcars-news/462.html :

"William Mcdonough (Founder, McDounough & Partners Environmental Design): In the 70's Sheik Yamani speaking for OPEC in London said 'We will drop the price of oil, destroy those [alternative energy/conservation] investments on Wall Street, and then put the price of oil back. Which is exactly what they have done every single decade.' "

(9) *The Base Of The Pyramid Protocol: Toward Next Generation BOP Strategy* p5

(10) Tata Nano information adapted from BBC News
http://news.bbc.co.uk/1/hi/business/7180396.stm

(11) Adapted from http://www.theoildrum.com/node/3561

(12) Stephen Stirling *Linkingthinking* project in Scotland http://www.wwf.org.uk/core/about/scotland/sc_0000001453.asp

Chapter 5

(1) Rob Hopkins *The Transition Handbook: from oil dependency to local resilience* Green Books (2007)
http://transitionculture.org/shop/the-transition-handbook/

(2) http://www.learning-org.com/97.07/0193.html

(3) John Miller, *The holistic curriculum*, Ontario, OISE Press (1988) and in *Greenprints for Changing Schools*, S.Greig, D.Selby and G.Pike, WWF/Kogan Page (1989)

(4) Cradle to Cradle Design certification http://www.c2ccertified.com/

(5) See for example Dora Marinova, David Annandale *The International Handbook on Environmental Technology Management.* Edward Elgar Publishing (2006) p33-35

A 575 page resource for more detailed discussion on industrial ecology, biomimicry and green chemistry

(6) Permaculture information and links from the Permaculture Magazine http://www.permaculture-info.co.uk/

(7) *Organic agriculture and the global food supply* Catherine Badgley et al in Renewable Agriculture and Food Systems (2007), 22:86-108 Cambridge University Press

"The principal objections to the proposition that organic agriculture can contribute significantly to the global food supply are low yields and insufficient quantities of organically acceptable fertilizers... Model estimates indicate that organic methods could produce enough food on a global per capita basis to sustain the current human population, and potentially an even larger population, without increasing the agricultural land base."

(8) George Chan in his own words http://www.scizerinm.org/chanarticle.html

(9) Dream Farm 2 and more from Mae–Wan Ho. *Dream Farm 2 – a proposal. How to beat climate change and post fossil fuel economy*. Institute of Science in Society (2006).

Also see http://www.i-sis.org.uk/DreamFarm2.php

(10) Models for Vertical Farm http://www.verticalfarm.com/Default.aspx

Benefits claimed:

Year-round crop production; 1 indoor acre is equivalent to 4-6 outdoor acres or more, depending upon the crop (e.g., strawberries: 1 indoor acre=30 outdoor acres)

No weather-related crop failures due to droughts, floods, pests

All VF food is grown organically: no herbicides, pesticides, or fertilizers

VF virtually eliminates agricultural runoff by recycling black water

VF returns farmland to nature, restoring ecosystem functions and services

Chapter notes and references

VF greatly reduces the incidence of many infectious diseases that are acquired at the agricultural interface

VF converts black and gray water into potable water by collecting the water of evapotranspiration

VF adds energy back to the grid via methane generation from composting non-edible parts of plants and animals

VF dramatically reduces fossil fuel use (no tractors, ploughs, shipping.)

VF converts abandoned urban properties into food production centers

VF creates sustainable environments for urban centers

VF creates new employment opportunities

(11) More on the low key approach. http://skyvegetables.wordpress.com/ A veritable cornucopia of ideas about urban agriculture

(12) Yale's Gus Speth calls for shift from U.S. consumer capitalism to solve environmental woes http://www.eenews.net/tv/transcript/786

(13) c.f. Bonnett, M *Education for Sustainability as a Frame of Mind*, Environmental Education. Research, 8.1, pp. 9–20, (2002)

(14) A wealth of short films on sustainable development issues are downloadable at http://www.green.tv Short films featuring leading sustainability thinkers and practitioners are to be found on http://www.bigpicture.tv

The immensely popular animation the StoryofStuff chronicles the unsustainable nature of our world with panache – before leading briefly onto the closed loop model. http://www.storyofstuff.com

For free colour still images to download to use in educational institutions visit the UK Government's Sustainable Schools website http://www.teachernet.gov.uk/sustainableschools/ and Yorkshire&Humber ESD Forum website http://www.yorkshireandhumber.net/esd. For ideas on how to use these images in the classroom download Cathy Midwinter's '*Using internet images for ESD*' (2008) publication at Y&H ESD Forum website. For stunning high resolution images of Earth from space use NASA photos–they are copyright free and can be used in education institutions http://earthobservatory.nasa.gov/Newsroom/NewImages/images_index.php3

For everything else on Living Machines, McDonough, Braungart, Benyus and Lovins try Bioneers, YouTube, Flickr or Google Video.

Chapter 6

(1) This 'school and college in transition' illustration indicates the potential to engage religious groups with the development of eco-restorative schools and colleges. The Alliance of Religions and Conservation (ARC) works with 11 faiths world wide. Each faith has its own distinctive history and teachings, and its own unique relationship with the natural world. The ARC is working in partnership with the following religions: Baha'i, Buddhism, Christianity, Daoism, Hinduism, Islam, Jainism, Judaism, Shintoism, Sikism, Zoroastrianism.

Example:

"... A result of Buddhist practice is that one does not feel that one's existence is so much more important than anyone else's. The notions of ego clinging, the importance of the individual and emphasis on self is, in the West, a dominant outlook which is moving to the East as "development" and consumerism spread. Instead of looking at things as a seamless undivided whole we tend to categorize and compartmentalize. Instead of seeing nature as our great teacher we waste and do not replenish and forget that Buddha learned his "wisdom from nature." Once we treat nature as our friend, to cherish it, then we can see the need to change from the attitude of dominating nature to an attitude of working with nature – we are an intrinsic part of all existence rather than seeing ourselves as in control of it."

From *Faith in Conservation* by Martin Palmer with Victoria Finlay, (World Bank 2003). The ARC website outlines the basics of each faith's history, beliefs and teachings on ecology
http://www.arcworld.org/faiths.htm

(2) *Web 2.0 and the changing ways we are using computers for learning: what are the implications for pedagogy and curriculum?* Graham Attwell, Director, Pontydysgu.
http://www.elearningeuropa.info/files/media/media13018.pdf

Chapter 7

(1) Why? As discussed in several chapters prices must reflect the full social and environmental costs to work effectively in a market – prices are messages. Al Gore favours a carbon tax which is revenue neutral–balanced by removing taxes on people (income tax) so that

overall tax take remains constant. There are other approaches including carbon trading. See *Sense and Sustainability* online for teaching support in this arena.

NB See the presentation by Al Gore and also one by Amory Lovins on the Technology Entertainment Design (TED) website. http://www.ted.com/ A must visit site for general studies and the ideas circulating in *Sense and Sustainability*. Incudes Michael Pollan on food, William McDonough on cradle to cradle, Norman Foster on the green agenda, Janine Benyus on biomimicry and Alex Steffen on sustainable futures. A one stop briefing site in moving pictures!

(2) Charles Krebs *The Ecological World View* CSIRO (2008)

(3) Philosphy for Children at http://www.sapere.net/

(4) His *Climate Change Knowledge in a Nutshell* is highly recommended. http://www.pik-potsdam.de/infodesk

(5) Jim Hansen is perhaps the world's leading climate scientist and widely reported. http://www.columbia.edu/~jeh1/

(6) TREC, Trans Mediterranean Renewable Energy Coalition. A Club of Rome initiative see http://www.desertec.org/

(7) http://www.oilendgame.com/ If you download consider a donation? It was a $1 million dollar research project. See also TED above.

List of figures

Chapter notes and references

About the authors

Ken Webster is a teacher, workshop facilitator, trainer and author. He works internationally as an educational consultant specialising in ESD and communicating ideas about sustainability. He has authored over 15 books and designed interactive exhibitions in St Petersburg and Moscow. A musician in his spare time he lives in rural Wales.

Craig Johnson is an ecologist. He is currently Yorkshire&Humber Region ESD co-ordinator, working with the regional development agency, Government Office, schools and other stakeholders to develop regionally distinctive teacher training programmes linked to the UK Government's National Sustainable Schools framework.

From 1990 to 2002, Craig was head of secondary education at WWF UK. During this time, Craig and Ken worked together extensively with industry partners on collaborative education projects related to sustainable development – this included the development of WWF's business and environment scholarship scheme with British Airways, BAA plc, ICI/Tioxide and B&Q/Kingfisher.

Lightning Source UK Ltd.
Milton Keynes UK
UKOW05f0445070915

258172UK00004B/239/P

9 780955 983108